the Quiltmakers

Consultant Pam Lintott

D&C
David and Charles
www.rucraft.co.uk

A DAVID & CHARLES BOOK
Copyright © David & Charles Limited 2009

David & Charles is an F+W Media Inc. company
4700 East Galbraith Road
Cincinnati, OH 45236

First published in the UK and US in 2009

Text and designs copyright © Lynette Anderson-O'Rourke, Janet Bolton, Lynne Edwards, Joanna Figueroa,
Carolyn Forster, Lynette Jensen, Marsha McCloskey and Petra Prins 2009
Layout and photography copyright © David & Charles 2009

A catalogue record for this book is available from the
British Library.

ISBN: 978-0-7153-3173-6 hardback
ISBN: 978-0-7153-3174-3 paperback

Printed in China by RR Donnelley
for David & Charles
Brunel House   Newton Abbot   Devon

Commissioning Editor Jane Trollope
Consultant Pam Lintott
Editor Verity Muir
Project Editor Lin Clements
Art Editor Sarah Clark
Production Controller Kelly Smith

Visit our website at www.davidandcharles.co.uk

David & Charles books are available from all good
bookshops; alternatively you can contact our Orderline
on 0870 9908222 or write to us at FREEPOST EX2
110, D&C Direct, Newton Abbot, TQ12 4ZZ (no stamp
required UK only); US customers call 800-289-0963
and Canadian customers call 800-840-5220.

Contents

Introduction
by Pam Lintott

I opened The Quilt Room back in 1981 and from the beginning teaching the art of patchwork and quilting has been a priority. We have held classes in our workshop above the shop for many years and tutors have come from all over the country to teach there. It has been a great privilege to get to know so many talented people. In 1992 our book *The Quilt Room Patchwork & Quilting Workshops* was published. Each chapter was written as a workshop by a different tutor who had taught at The Quilt Room. It was an amazing success as people living too far to attend one of our classes could now have a personal tutorial in their own home! Since the publication of that book many more talented quilters have taught at The Quilt Room and there are many more that we haven't yet had. Here lies the beauty of this book…

Lynette Anderson-O'Rourke

Australia is the home of so many talented quilters and Lynette is up there among the top. I love her style of patchwork, which combines primitive folk art with a traditional country look. She has produced many gorgeous patterns and our recent block of the month programme designed by Lynette was a great success. You will find her project in this book is full of interesting techniques, all explained in easy steps.

Janet Bolton

Janet is known worldwide for her naïve appliqué. I am privileged to have one of her farmyard scenes hanging in my house and everyone admires it. She puts together such simple shapes and designs but the overall effect is far from simple – how does she do it? We have been lucky enough to have Janet teach at The Quilt Room quite often but we are always getting phone calls asking the date of the next Janet Bolton workshop. We no longer name her workshop Naïve Appliqué but just call it 'A Day with Janet Bolton'.

What if I had a magic wand and could conjure up a selection of tutors from all over the world – people who have inspired me and I know would inspire you? Well, this book is just that magic wand. Without moving from the comfort of your own home, you can dip into workshops from the most talented quiltmakers from all over the world – what luxury! Without travelling any distance you can attend eight different workshops covering a wide range of quiltmaking skills and you will without doubt enjoy the talent that exudes from these pages. If you don't attend another workshop in your life, grab this book and don't let it go. The tutors here are quilters from all over the world who have contributed so much to the art of patchwork and quilting and who have certainly been an inspiration to me.

Lynne Edwards

What can I say about Lynne? She is a much-loved teacher, well respected all over the world, and her infectious sense of humour is well known. When I received news of her being given the MBE and saw a photo of her receiving it from HRH The Prince of Wales I felt such a sense of pride that I actually knew this talented quilter. We have been lucky enough to have Lynne teach at The Quilt Room and her workshops are always full to overflowing – such is her following. Her quilts using cathedral window patchwork are well known and she has won many awards for them. In this workshop she teaches perspective and for those wishing to take their patchwork and quilting to another level this is the workshop for you.

Joanna Figueroa

When I saw the first range of fabrics designed by Joanna for Moda Fabrics I immediately fell in love with them. That creamy vintage look was gorgeous and just what I was looking for. Every range since then has been just as beautiful and just as irresistible, all having such a wonderful warmth that you can't wait to get your hands on the fabrics and start quilting. To have a workshop on colour from this talented designer is such a treat – so just sit down, relax and enjoy it.

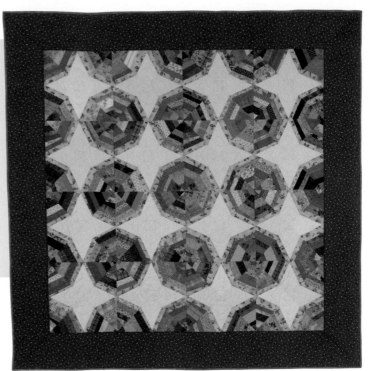

Carolyn Forster

I consider Carolyn to be one of the most talented quiltmakers in the UK at the moment. She has a fantastic eye for colour and design and her quilts always look stunning. We were extremely lucky to have her work at The Quilt Room for many years and she still teaches many classes for us, including our beginners, intermediates and advanced. Her knowledge of all aspects of quiltmaking is second to none and her love of the art of patchwork and quilting and her enthusiasm for imparting her knowledge is a joy.

Lynette Jensen

I don't think there is a quilter out there who is not familiar with the Thimbleberries books and fabrics. I have stocked them in the shop for years and they are as popular today as they ever were. Lynette is always bringing out new patterns, books and fabrics that reflect the current trends but I always associate her with country-style quilts using a palette of reds, greens and golds. A few years ago we were thrilled to have Lynette visit us at The Quilt Room and we organized an 'At Home with Lynette' day. She was inundated with people wanting to meet her and by the end of the day she had virtually lost her voice – such is her reputation.

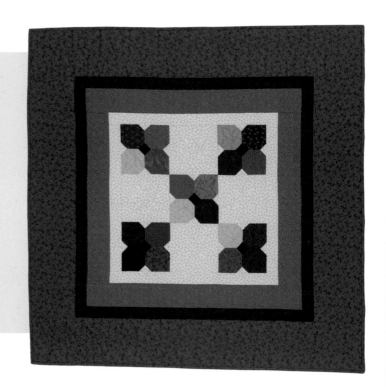

Marsha McCloskey

I have always admired the accuracy of Marsha's quilts. I stocked her book *Feathered Star Quilts* when it came out in 1987 and loved it so much that I took it home and vowed that one day I would make a Feathered Star quilt. I am embarrassed to say that I never did make one but hey… there's plenty of time. I doubt whether mine would look quite so perfect as Marsha's but I can live in hope. A few years ago Marsha visited the UK to teach Feathered Star at a weekend convention in the UK. Several ladies who work at The Quilt Room attended and loved Marsha's calm and patient teaching of how to draft this complex pattern in the simplest of terms. They were all so inspired. My regret is that I didn't manage to lure her to Dorking to teach a workshop for us.

Petra Prins

I first met Petra when we both had booths at the Festival of Quilts in Birmingham, UK. My regular customers kept coming up and telling me about the beautiful reproduction fabrics they had found, so off I went to investigate and met the lovely Petra. Her booth looked just beautiful and she had some gorgeous quilts hanging up which she very kindly let me photograph. Later that year when we bumped into each other at Quilt Market in Houston she laughed when I showed her my mobile telephone and there as my screensaver was a picture of her quilts. Petra loves medallion quilts and I just love the way she blends her fabrics together to create just the perfect effect I look for in a quilt.

Richly Coloured Traditions
by Lynette Jensen, USA

My approach to quiltmaking for the past thirty-plus years has stayed the same, that the process should be enjoyable and do-able. As a self-taught quilter, I was attracted to the traditional quilt designs that basically used triangles, squares and rectangles of various sizes in many varieties of colours and prints – the more the better. The antique quilts that I loved and started collecting, were simply pieced, but the combination of fabrics was the attraction. I have also always loved the texture of a quilt, both to the eye and to the touch. For many early quilters, quilting was a function of need and economy and scrap quilts have become a staple for all quilters. They rank among my favourites as well.

There are two projects in this chapter; the first (shown opposite) is a wall quilt that could also be used as a throw or table-topper. It can be made by a beginner quilter but also be an enjoyable project for an experienced quilter. Coordinated scraps are perfect for the flower blocks, surrounded by a border fabric that pulls them altogether.

For those who like even smaller quilts, directions for a miniature quilt are also included in this chapter on page 16. There is always a spot in any décor for a little quilt, full of colour and lovingly stitched. These small quilts are particularly nice when professionally framed as they take on a new level of importance and ease of display. Both projects are machine quilted using simple stencils that I have designed for the hand or machine quilter (see page 117 for availability details).

"I have always loved the texture of a quilt, both to the eye and to the touch."

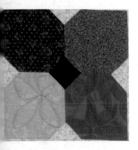

Wall quilts that can be used as throws or table-toppers are very popular and for those with limited space or time, this quilt is the perfect project. See page 16 for a mini version.

Lynette Jensen Inspirations

The traditional Thimbleberries palette started with combinations of rich earth hues of reds, greens, golds, browns and black, which very much replicated the antique quilts to which I was attracted. They were also the colours I used when decorating my home.

The best thing about quilting, however, is the wonderful range of colours in beautiful fabrics in the market place, so a simple quilt design can be made in vastly different fabrics and colour ranges to produce a quilt that is just right for every quilt maker. The various Thimbleberries fabric ranges I design now reflect the traditional Thimbleberries palette, plus light and bright ranges as well as holiday themes.

Embracing all the wonderful fabrics at their disposal, modern quilt makers have expanded the craft into far more than bed quilts. Most popular are wall quilts that can also be used as table-toppers and decorative quilts for beds to coordinate with a larger quilt.

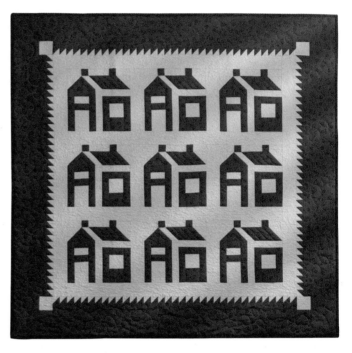

Bachelor Buttons is shown here in a more traditional colour palette of softened and subdued hues with a floral border, illustrating how versatile this pattern is and how dramatically the appearance of a quilt changes with a different collection of fabrics.

Traditional patterns and fabrics have long been the mainstay of the Thimbleberries fabric and pattern collections. Variations of the Little Red Houses quilt shown here have been a favourite of quilters for decades. As old as the design is, it is interesting that it has such a graphic quality and would be a wonderful decorative accessory for a contemporary setting as well as a traditional environment. This pattern can be found in the book *Basic Beauties Big and Small* by Thimbleberries (see Additional Reading page 117).

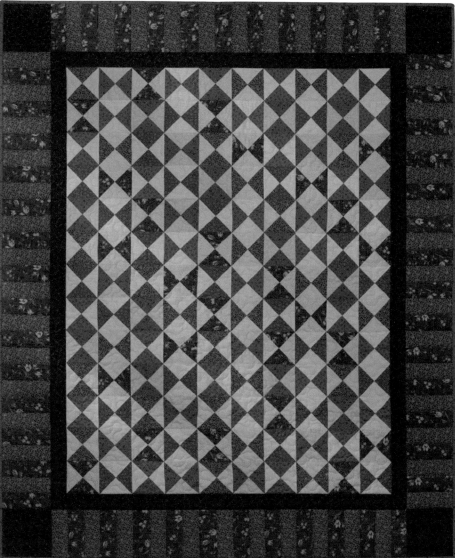

The Everyday Quilt is ready for just that – everyday use. It is the perfect size to be used as a throw for a quick cover up when a chill is in the air. The abundance of fabrics used is reminiscent of a scrap quilt and gives the quilt a casual, less formal appearance. The pattern for this quilt can be found in the book, *Basic Beauties Big and Small* by Thimbleberries (see page 117).

Choosing the Fabric

Selecting fabrics for a quilt project is the most fun part of making a quilt for some, although for others it is a daunting task. I think the secret is to practise. The more you do, the more confident you will become in making your own fabric selections.

For the very beginner, it is sometimes easiest to start with a simple two-colour quilt, such as Little Red Houses (opposite), so all attention can be paid to the piecing process. The next step would be to select a multicoloured print, such as the floral shown opposite in the traditional colourway sample of the Bachelor Buttons quilt. Once the floral print has been selected, pull all other colour references for various parts of the quilt from that one focal fabric. If it is a large print, it is very often used in the border and maybe repeated in other larger pattern pieces in the quilt. The other coordinating fabrics will visually pull the quilt together. It is also important to include a variety of print sizes so all parts of the quilt have their own character, yet combine nicely to create a harmonious quilt.

Batchelor Buttons Wall Quilt

This quilt can be displayed as a wall quilt or used as a small throw or table-topper. It can be made by a beginner quilter but also be an enjoyable project for an experienced quilter. Coordinated scraps are perfect for the flower blocks, surrounded by a border fabric that pulls them altogether. The instructions are for the bright colourway but a more traditional palette of colours could be used – refer to the box below for colours. This quilt is made in the same way as the mini version on page 16 (see Fig 1 overleaf for the layout). The projects were machine quilted using simple stencils (available from Thimbleberries – see page 117). The project was designed using imperial measurements and although metric equivalents have been provided, the best results will be obtained using imperial.

Size of finished quilt: 56in x 56in (142.2cm x 142.2cm).

Materials (for the bright colourway)

The yardage given for the project is based on 44in (111.7cm) wide fabric and is more than adequate for the project. To make the traditional colourway see the box below for colours

- Twenty 5½in (14cm) medium-print squares for flower blocks (½yd/m total)
- Beige print for flower blocks, alternate blocks and inner border ¾yd (0.75m)
- Black print for flower centres ⅛yd (0.125m)
- Green print for wide middle border ⅝yd (0.6m)
- Red print for narrow middle border ⅜yd (0.3m)
- Blue print for outer border (cut on the lengthwise grain) 1¾yd (0.75m)
- Backing fabric 3½yd (3.25m)
- Wadding (batting) at least 62in x 62in (158cm x 158cm)
- Binding fabric ⅝yd (0.6m) of a blue print
- Quilting threads as desired

The Batchelor Buttons quilt can be made in the bright colourway shown opposite or in the more traditional shades shown on page 10. The instructions are for the bright colourway but it is easy to substitute the alternate colours given here.

Bright Colourway
Beige print
Black print
Green print
Red print
Blue print

Traditional Colourway
Beige print
Black/brown print
Light brown print
Green print
Brown/rose floral print

"This bright colourway of the Bachelor Buttons Quilt is a graphic representation of easy, traditional piecing – perfect for a beginner quilter or a busy experienced quilter. The three plain borders draw attention to the colourful centre of the quilt, just as a mat and frame does to a piece of art."

Fig 1 Quilt layout

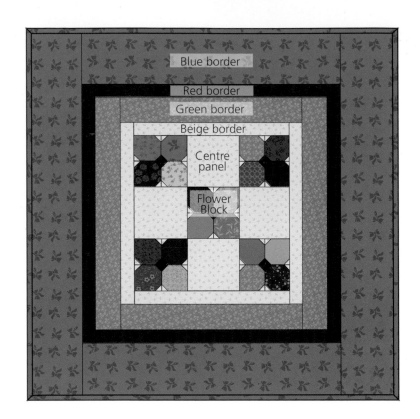

Blue border

Red border

Green border

Beige border

Centre panel

Flower Block

Making the flower blocks

1 Cut sufficient pieces for five flower blocks as follows.
From the 5½in (14cm) medium print squares cut twenty 4½in (11.43cm) squares for the flower blocks.
From beige print cut two 1½in x 44in strips (3.8cm x 11.76cm) and from these strips cut forty 1½in (3.8cm) squares.
From black print cut one 1½in x 44in (3.8cm x 11.76cm) strip and from this strip cut twenty 1½in (3.8cm) squares for the flower centres.

2 With right sides together, position 1½in (3.8cm) beige squares on two opposite corners of a 4½in (11.43cm) medium print square. Draw a diagonal line on each beige square and then stitch along this line (see Fig 2). Trim seam allowances on these units to ¼in (6mm) and then press.

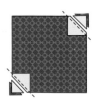

Fig 2   make 20

3 With right sides together, position a 1½in (3.8cm) black square on the corner of each of the units. Draw a diagonal line on the black square and stitch on the line (Fig 3). Trim the seam allowance to ¼in (6mm) and then press.

Fig 3   make 20

4 Sew the units together in pairs and press. Sew the pairs together to make a flower block and press (Fig 4). Make five blocks in total. Each block should measure 8½in (21.6cm) square.

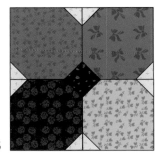

Fig 4 Flower block – make 5

Making the quilt centre

1 From beige print cut one 8½in x 44in (21.6cm x 111.7cm) strip. From this strip cut four 8½in (21.6cm) blocks.

2 Sew together the flower blocks and the 8½in (21.6cm) beige squares in three horizontal rows as in Fig 5. Press seam allowances toward the beige blocks.

3 Pin the three rows at the block intersections and then sew the rows together. Press the seam allowances in one direction. At this point the quilt centre should measure 24½in (62.2cm) square.

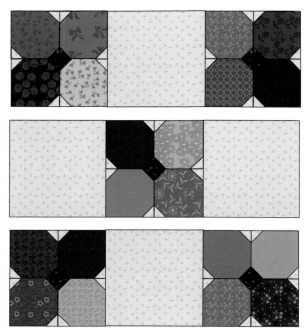

Fig 5

Adding the borders

1 The yardage given for borders allows for wide outer border strips to be cut on the lengthwise grain (a few extra inches are allowed for trimming). The yardage given allows for narrow border strips to be cut on the crosswise grain (see page 52 for further information on fabric grain). Diagonally piece the border strips as needed – see technique on page 110.

2 From beige print cut four 2½in x 44in (6.3cm x 111.7cm) inner border strips.
From green print cut four 4½in x 44in (11.4cm x 111.7cm) wide middle border strips.
From red print cut four 2½in x 44in (6.3cm x 111.7cm) narrow middle border strips.
From blue print (cut on the lengthwise grain) cut two 8½in x 63in (21.6cm x 160cm) side outer border strips and then cut two 8½in x 44in (21.6cm x 111.7cm) top/bottom outer border strips.

3 Mark the centre points along all four sides of the quilt with pins. For the top and bottom borders, measure the quilt through the middle as this will be the most accurate measurement to achieve a 'square' quilt. Measure the sides of the quilt in the same manner.

4 Attach the 2½in (6.3cm) wide beige inner border strips to the quilt top, attaching the top and bottom strips first. Trim off excess fabric and then attach the side strips.

5 Continue to add the other borders, attaching the green border strips, the red border strips and then the blue outer border strips. When attaching the last two side border strips, taking a few backstitches at the beginning and end of the border will help keep quilt borders intact during quilting.

Finishing the quilt

1 Cut a 3½yd (3.25m) length of backing fabric in half crosswise to make two 1¾yd (1.6m) lengths. Sew the long edges together with ¼in (6mm) seams and press (Fig 6). Trim the backing and wadding (batting) so they are 6in (15.2cm) larger than the quilt top.

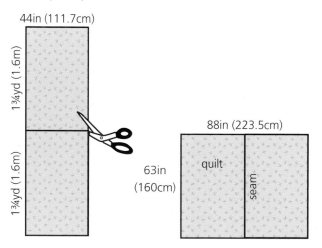

Fig 6

2 Mark the quilt top for quilting – see suggestions below. Make a quilt sandwich of the backing, wadding and quilt top (see page 112). Hand tack (baste) the layers together to secure them for hand quilting.

Quilting suggestions

Thimbleberries quilt stencils by Quilting Creations International are available from quilt shops or visit www.quiltingcreations.com
Flower blocks – TB9 7in radish top.
Beige alternate blocks – TB20 7in tulip, with stipple behind.
Beige inner border – stipple.
Green wide middle border – TB91 3½in fence.
Red narrow middle border – TB64 1½in Nordic scroll.
Blue outer border – TB43, 7in star vine border.

3 When quilting is complete, remove tacking (basting). Hand tack (baste) the layers together a scant ¼in (6mm) from the edge – this keeps layers from shifting and prevents puckers from forming when adding the binding. Trim excess wadding and backing fabric even with the edge of the quilt top. From blue print cut six 2¾in x 44in (7cm x 111.7cm) strips and bind the quilt as described on page 114.

Mini Batchelor Buttons

This half-size version of the Batchelor Buttons design is perfect for a table-topper and would be ideal for a beginner quilter. It is made in the same way as the larger version shown on page 13. The project was designed using imperial measurements and although metric equivalents have been provided, the best results will be obtained using imperial.

Size of finished quilt: 28in x 28in (71cm x 71cm).

Materials

- Twenty medium-print squares for flower blocks (2½in/6.3cm squares – ¼yd/m in total)
- Beige print for flower blocks, alternate blocks and inner border ⅓yd (0.3m)
- Black print for flower centres ⅛yd (0.125m)
- Green print for wide middle border ¼yd (0.25m)
- Rose print for narrow middle border ⅛yd (0.125m)
- Blue print for outer border ½yd (0.5m)
- Backing fabric 1yd (1m)
- Wadding (batting) 1yd (1m)
- Binding fabric ⅓yd (0.3m) of a blue print
- Quilting threads as desired

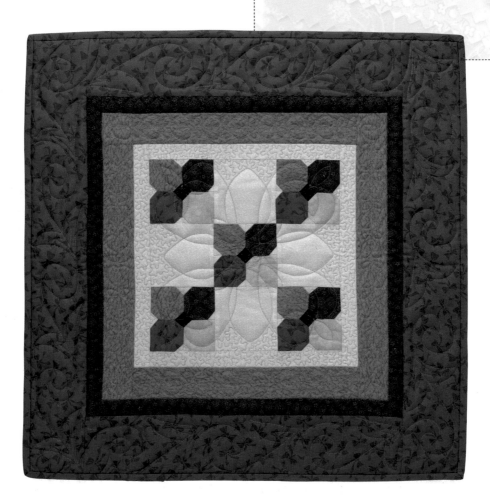

Making the flower blocks

1 Cut sufficient pieces for five flower blocks as follows.
From medium-print squares cut twenty 2½in (6.35cm) squares for the flower blocks.
From beige print cut one 1in x 44in strip (2.5cm x 11.7cm) and from this strip cut forty 1in (2.5cm) squares.
From black print cut one 1in x 44in strip (2.5cm x 11.7cm) and from this strip cut twenty 1in (2.5cm) squares for the flower centres.

2 Piece a flower block together as follows. With right sides together, position 1in (2.5cm) beige squares on two opposite corners of a 2½in (6.35cm) medium print square. Draw a diagonal line on each beige square and then stitch along this line (see Fig 1). Trim seam allowances on these units to ¼in (6mm) and press.

Fig 1

make 20

3 With right sides together, position a 1in (2.5cm) black square on the corner of each of the units. Draw a diagonal line on the black square and stitch on the line (Fig 2). Trim the seam allowance to ¼in (6mm) and then press.

Fig 2   make 20

4 Sew the units together in pairs and press. Sew the pairs together to make a flower block and press (Fig 3). Make five flower blocks in total. At this point each flower block should measure 4½in (11.43cm) square.

Fig 3 Flower block – make 5

Making the quilt centre

1 From beige print cut one 4½in x 44in (11.43cm x 111.7cm) strip. From this strip cut four 4½in (11.43cm) alternate blocks.

2 Sew together the flower blocks and the 4½in (11.4cm) beige alternate block squares in three horizontal rows (see Fig 5 on page 15). Press seam allowances toward the beige alternate blocks.

3 Pin the three rows at the block intersections and sew the rows together. Press the seam allowances in one direction. At this point the quilt centre should measure 12½in (31.75cm) square.

Adding the borders

1 The yardage given allows for borders to be cut on the crosswise grain. Diagonally piece strips as needed – see instructions for creating these strips on page 110. From beige print cut two 1½in x 44in (3.8cm x 111.7cm) inner border strips.

From green print cut two 2½in x 44in (6.35cm x 111.7cm) wide middle border strips.
From rose print cut two 1½in x 44in (3.8cm x 111.7cm) narrow middle border strips.
From blue print cut three 4½in x 44in (11.43cm x 111.7cm) outer border strips.

2 Mark the centre points along all four sides of the quilt with pins. For the top and bottom borders, measure the quilt through the middle as this measurement will be the most accurate to achieve a 'square' quilt. Measure the sides of the quilt in the same manner.

3 Attach the 1½in (3.8cm) wide beige inner border strips to the quilt top, attaching the top and bottom strips first. Trim off excess fabric and then attach the side strips. In the same manner add the green, then the red and then the blue borders.

Finishing the quilt

1 Trim the backing and wadding (batting) so they are 6in (15.2in) larger than the quilt top. Mark the quilt top for quilting – see suggestions below. Make a quilt sandwich of the backing, wadding and quilt top (see page 112). Hand tack (baste) the layers together to secure them for hand quilting.

Quilting suggestions

Thimbleberries quilt stencils by Quilting Creations International are available from quilt shops or visit www.quiltingcreations.com
Flower quilt centre – TB87 11½in heart swirl.
Beige floating inner border – stipple.
Green wide middle border – TB67 1½in heart chain.
Red narrow middle border – in the ditch.
Blue outer border – TB65 3½in Nordic scroll.

2 When quilting is complete, remove tacking (basting). Trim the excess wadding and backing fabric even with the edge of the quilt top. From blue print cut three 2¾in x 44in (7cm x 111.7cm) strips and finish by binding the quilt as described on page 114.

"The large plain border in a tonal print on this quilt is the perfect canvas to showcase beautiful hand or machine quilting."

Medallion Traditions
by Petra Prins, The Netherlands

My love of colour and fabrics began very early and sewing became not only necessary but a natural part of my life. As a child I made clothes for my dolls, then myself and later for my four children. I didn't come in contact with patchwork until the late 1980s, although some years before I had been sewing squares together to make a cover for a sofa not realizing that this was a form of patchwork. When my sister-in-law visited us from America she brought a stack of fabrics and a pattern. We called the fabric 'American cotton' and the first block I made was a pinwheel. At this time I was busy starting a shop, designing, making and selling clothing made from natural fabrics like wool, silk, and cotton. I often worked with cottons from Liberty of London, and even today I'm drawn to their traditional designs and colours.

The year 2000 brought the chance to move my shop to bigger premises in a city and I grasped the opportunity with both hands. During visits to America, where my husband lived and worked for a time, I came into contact with patchwork again, discovering not just newly made quilts but antique quilts. Finding reproduction 19th century fabrics awoke something in me – this was what I was waiting for, a new way forward. So I got out of the clothes business, began finding wholesalers selling reproduction fabrics and bought my first antique quilt.

Of all the antique quilt styles, my favourite are the English medallion quilts. In the medallion design shown opposite I enjoyed using the border prints and stripes in different ways. The large-scale prints give this quilt the 'antique' look that I so love and hope you do too.

"The antique quilts I love the most are the English medallion quilts, where all the fabric remnants are worked around the centre."

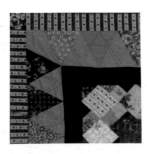

I chose to feature a medallion quilt for this book to show how well the design works with antique-style fabrics. The quilt is made from Japanese reproduction fabrics with a large rose border design as the focal point. Bep Wissels machine pieced and hand quilted this piece and it is called Julia's Quilt, after Bep's grand-daughter.

Petra Prins Inspirations

My interest in antique reproduction fabrics has grown since I opened my store in Zutphen in 2000. After buying my first antique quilt my hands itched to design my own quilts from these inspiring traditional fabrics. The discovery that Japanese manufacturers were producing antique French prints further inspired me as these fabrics were a perfect complement to the American reproductions I was already using. And my interest has grown again, for I have just purchased the Den Haan & Wagenmakers store in Amsterdam with my best friend Nel Kooiman. This store has been reproducing antique Dutch designs for more than twenty years. Making quilts combining English, American, French and Dutch reproduction fabrics is a wonderful new challenge. Shown here are some results of the combination of antique quilt style and Japanese and American reproduction fabrics.

This wall hanging, called Generation, is one of my favourites. Although I like to mix different fabric collections in my quilts, for this quilt I just used one line from Windham called Generation. It was the brick red combined with the wonderful blue that inspired me to make this medallion quilt with four Le Moyne stars in the middle.

The centre of this wall hanging, called Pastorale, is made from a French toile. The triangles around the centre block are made out of strips, the light pieces having an embroidered vine. The first border is made from the leftovers of the strips used for the triangles. The second border is a wonderful Japanese lace fabric and the outside border is a half-square triangle border.

This simple lap quilt has an eye-catching border and this wonderful rose print is not only used for the border but also in the centre of the star blocks. For the second framed border I again used a Japanese lace fabric with embroidery stitches.

Choosing the Fabric

Choosing fabrics for a quilt is one of my favourite things. I love rose prints and I used a lot in Julia's quilt, but I also love reproduction prints. I always look for fabric prints with more than two colours. When you have a blue fabric with a little red, pink, green and/or ecru, it matches wonderfully with a red fabric that contains the same colour shades. And for the rest, I let the fabrics and colours do the 'work'. Sometimes I hardly use any contrast, as you can see in Julia's quilt.

Julia's Quilt

This medallion quilt's focal point is a beautiful reproduction border print from a Japanese maker and scraps of my own collection of romantic floral fabrics. This traditional pattern is simple to make; it begins with a centre block with borders added one by one, and ends with the beautiful border print (see Fig 1 below for the quilt layout). Templates were used for the centre block and the pieced borders (provided on pages 29–31). The benefit of using templates is that you can easily use scraps of fabric. Quilting patterns are also provided. The project was designed using imperial measurements. For metric users this is not difficult at all, just buy yourself a good inch ruler, forget about centimetres and follow the instructions – it will work, you will see! Metric equivalents have been provided but the quilt really does work best if made in imperial inches.

Size of finished quilt: 56½in x 56½in (143.5cm x 143.5cm).

Materials
- Border fabric 1¾yd (1.6m) – I used a fabric with small and wide borders
- Contrast fabric for centre block (red dot in the quilt shown) 20in (50cm)
- Striped fabric for centre block and the 5th border (brown/ecru stripe) 16in (40cm)
- Neutral fabric for centre block and points in the 4th border 20in (50cm)
- Twelve or more fat eighths or assorted scraps of light, medium and dark fabric
- Wadding (batting) at least 60in x 60in (152.4cm x 152.4cm)
- Backing fabric at least 60in x 60in (152.4cm x 152.4cm)
- Binding fabric 16in (40cm) across the fabric width (or use the leftovers from your border fabric)
- Quilting threads as desired

Tip

I never wash my fabrics before I make a quilt but do after it's finished. Placing the quilt in the washing machine, I rinse it in tepid water with a large cup of ordinary salt, spin it and then put it in a medium-warm dryer for a few minutes. After that I lay it flat on a bed to dry. It then looks even more like an antique quilt.

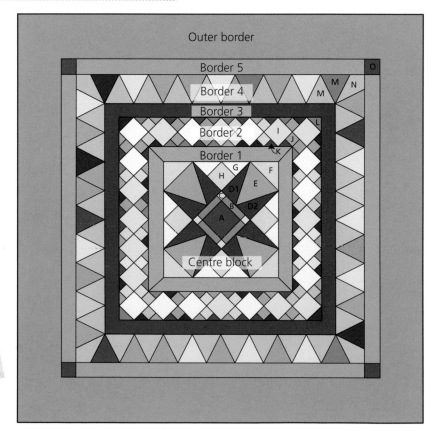

Fig 1 Quilt layout

"The dynamic of this quilt is that the design has dark and lights, which give movement, drawing the eye to different parts of the quilt. The design has the feel of an antique quilt, with stripes used where normally they would not be."

Making the centre block

1 The measurement of the centre block is 16in (40.6cm) square. Referring to the Fig 2 below, cut out the pieces using templates A, B, C, D1, D2, E, F, G and H, given full size on pages 29–30 (see also page 109 for advice on using templates). The number of pieces needed are given with the templates. Choose a rose pattern for template A. Note that templates D1 and D2 are mirrored.

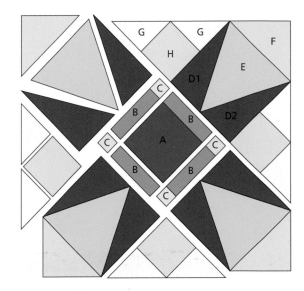

Fig 2 Piecing the centre block

2 Sew a piece B to either side of a piece A. Sew a piece C to either end of the remaining B pieces. Now sew these strips to the central BAB piece.

3 Sew two G pieces to one H piece to form a triangle. Make four of these units. Sew piece D1 to piece E and then to piece D2. Add piece F. Make four of these units.

4 Using Fig 2 as a guide and using ¼in (6mm) seams, sew the units together to form the centre block. See the Tip, right, for an alternate look for the centre block.

Tip

You can vary the look of the centre block by changing the tonal balance. Fig 3a shows how the block looks in the quilt, with dark star points. Fig 3b shows how the block would look with light star points.

Fig 3a   **Fig 3b**

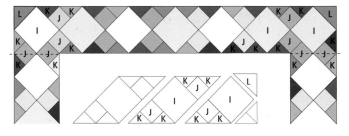

Making border 1

For this border I used the narrow border print stripe and mitred the corners. Cut four 2½in x 23in (6.35cm x 58.42cm) strips (it is always better to cut the strips longer for the borders with mitred corners). Pin each strip to the centre block beginning at the mid-point on each side, leaving extra at each end for the mitred corners. Sew the strips to the centre block, mitring the corners – see page 111. The quilt top should now measure 20½in x 20½in (52cm x 52cm).

Fig 4 Piecing border 2

Making border 2

1 Referring to Fig 4 below use templates I, J, K and L (given full size on page 31) and cut the following pieces.

From assorted light fabrics cut twenty-four squares using template I.

From assorted medium fabrics cut forty-eight squares using template J.

From assorted dark fabrics cut eighty-eight triangles using template K.

From dark fabric also cut four triangles using template L.

Sew the units together using Fig 4 as a guide (see Tip below).

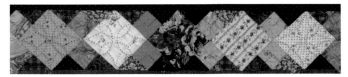

Tip

Petra hand pieced the corners of Border 2 using inset seams. You may find it easier when following Fig 4 to change the squares (Template J) on the corners to triangles (Template K) (shown at the dashed lines), which will make the piecing easier.

2 Now sew the border to the centre section. The top should now measure 28½in x 28½in (72.4cm x 72.4cm). I chose a lighter fabric for the squares and a darker for the triangles but you could reverse this to create a different effect – see Tip and Figs 5a and 5b below.

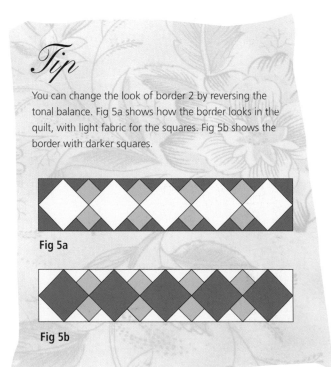

Tip

You can change the look of border 2 by reversing the tonal balance. Fig 5a shows how the border looks in the quilt, with light fabric for the squares. Fig 5b shows the border with darker squares.

Fig 5a

Fig 5b

Making border 3

For this border I used the same fabric as the points of the centre star. Cut four 2½in x 35in strips (6.35cm x 89cm). These measurements are longer because the corners are mitred on this border. Sew this border to the quilt. The quilt top should now measure 32½in x 32½in (82.55cm x 82.55cm).

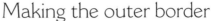

Making border 4

1 This border is made up of triangles with special attention given to the corners, creating a lively effect. Use templates M and N on page 31.

From neutral fabric cut thirty-two triangles using template M. From the assorted light, medium and dark scraps cut thirty-six triangles also using template M.

From the neutral fabric cut four triangles for the corners using template N. Sew the units together using Fig 6 as a guide.

2 Now sew the border to the centre section. The quilt top should now measure 40½in x 40½in (102.87cm x 102.87cm).

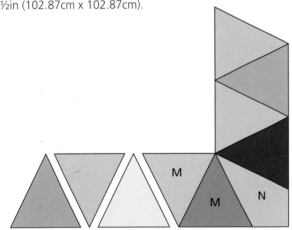

Fig 6 Piecing border 4

Making the outer border

From the length of the fabric cut four 6½in x 60in (16.5cm x 152.4cm) strips. These measurements are longer than the quilt top because the corners need to be mitred on this border. Don't worry if it is a bit narrower or wider than 6½in – your quilt will be just a little bit larger or smaller. Sew the border to the centre section, top and bottom strips first and then the side strips, and your quilt top is finished.

Tip

If using an attractive print fabric for a wide border, as my quilt did, look for a nice piece to centre so the fabric is shown to best advantage.

Making border 5

1 For this border I used the same striped fabric as for the triangles between the star points. Cut four 2½in x 40½in (6.35cm x 102.87cm) strips. Cut four 2in (5cm) squares using template O on page 31, using a contrasting fabric for these corner squares.

2 Sew two strips to the top and bottom of the quilt. Sew the 2in (5cm) squares to the two remaining strips and then sew these strips to the right and the left of the centre section, matching corner seams carefully.

Finishing the quilt

Layer the top, wadding (batting) and backing (see page 112). Quilt as you desire (see page 112) or use the quilt patterns we used, provided full size on pages 27–28. This quilt, like all the others in my store, is hand quilted. I know it's more time consuming but it's very relaxing and the final result always reminds me of an antique quilt. From the binding fabric cut six 2½in (6.3cm) strips and bind the quilt to finish (see page 114).

"Julia's Quilt is now finished – don't forget to sign and date it! I hope you enjoyed making this quilt as much as we did."

Julia's Quilt – quilting patterns

The quilting patterns here and overleaf are the ones I used for the quilt, or you could use your own ideas.

Quilting pattern for centre block

Quilting pattern for the squares in border 2

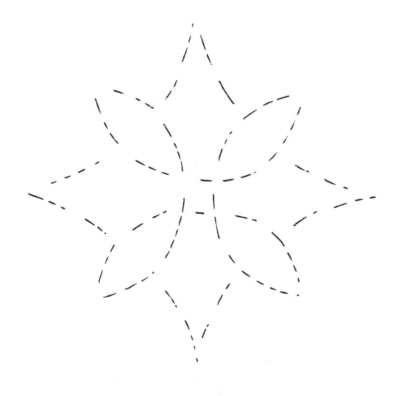

28

Quilting pattern (full size) for
outer border – repeat the
pattern as often as necessary
along the border

Julia's Quilt – templates

All templates are full size and ¼in (6mm) seam allowances are included. The dashed line indicates the cutting line and the straight line is the sewing line. Arrows indicate the fabric grain. Try to avoid cutting templates on the fabric bias – see Fig 2, page 52. See page 109 for using templates.

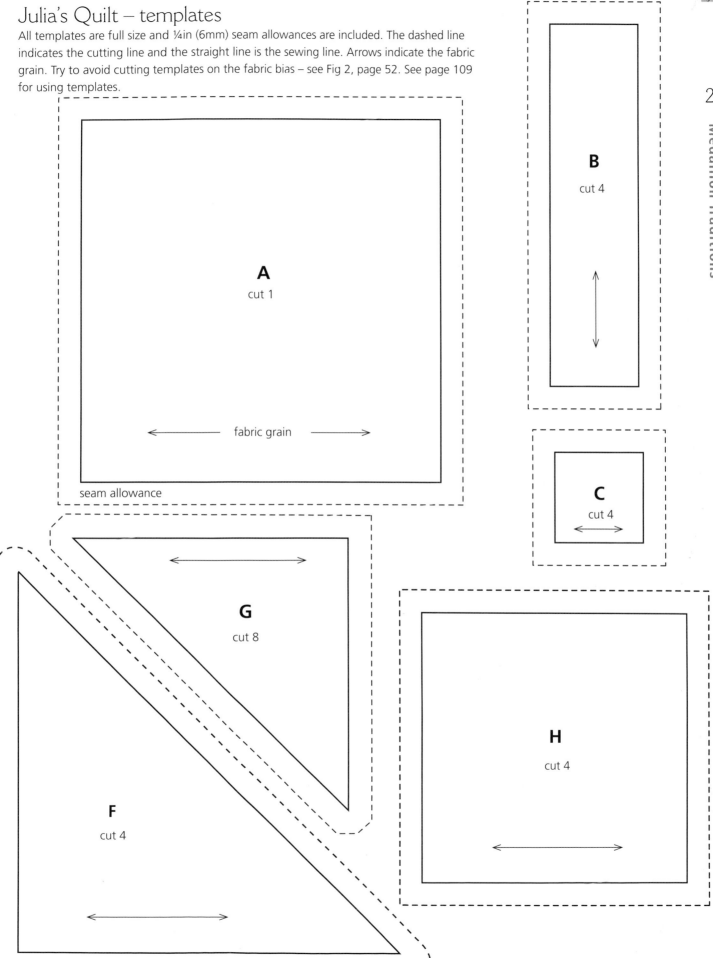

A
cut 1

fabric grain

seam allowance

B
cut 4

C
cut 4

G
cut 8

F
cut 4

H
cut 4

D1

cut 4

F

cut 4

D2

cut 4

E

cut 4

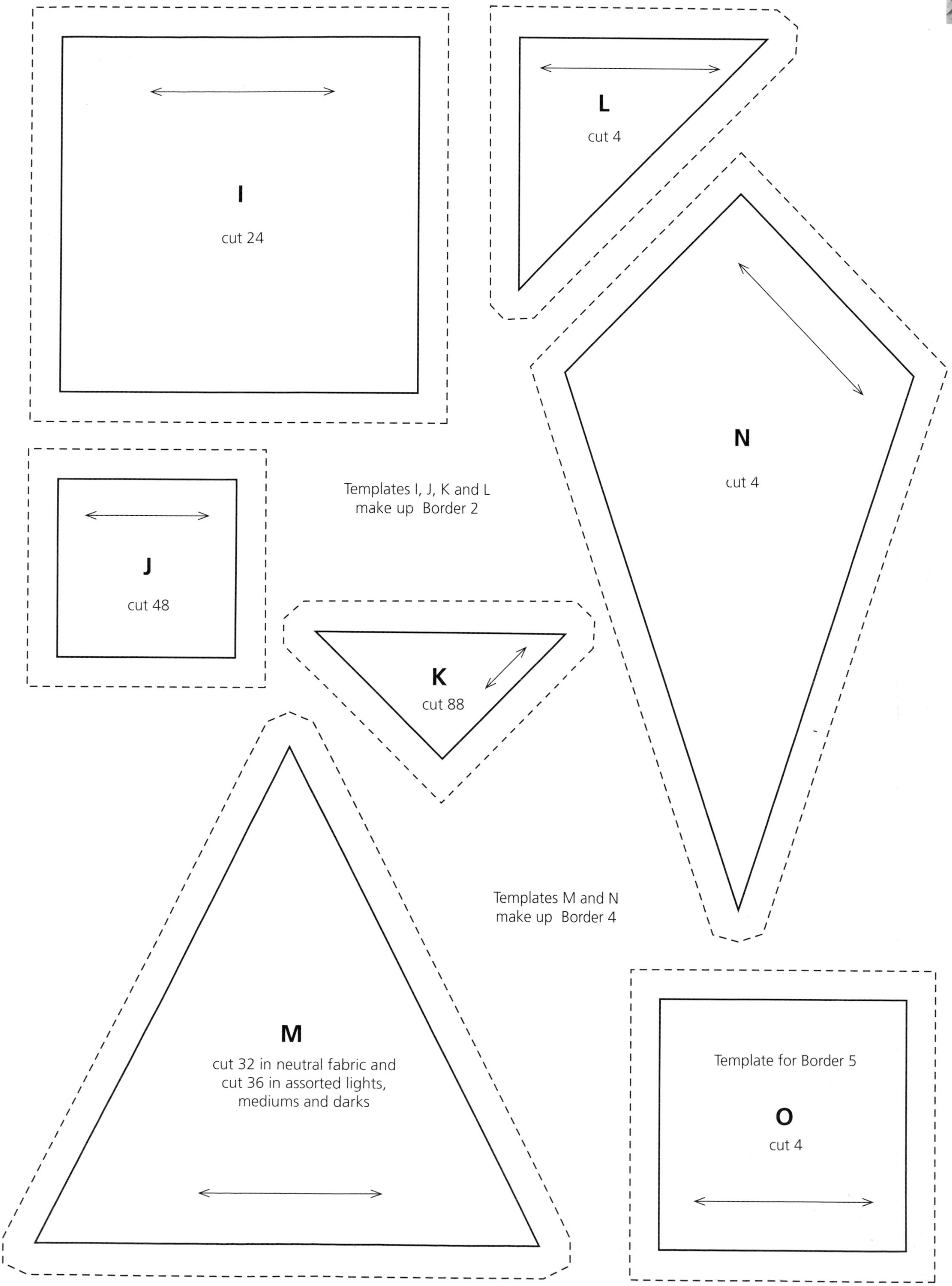

I

cut 24

L

cut 4

J

cut 48

Templates I, J, K and L
make up Border 2

K

cut 88

N

cut 4

Templates M and N
make up Border 4

M

cut 32 in neutral fabric and
cut 36 in assorted lights,
mediums and darks

Template for Border 5

O

cut 4

String Stars and Spiders' Webs
by Carolyn Forster, UK

I have always loved fabrics. I have always bought fabrics. It seems such a harmless way to indulge, because, after all, they can always be sewn into something useful – like a quilt. When I first started sewing in my teens I bought fabrics to sew my own clothes. My mother had sewn clothes for us as children so it was a natural progression that I would want to have a go. This also meant that we had a 'scrap bag' ready and waiting to be used in quilts. It did not take me long to realize that I could buy fabric for quilts to supplement the choice from the scrap bag and not bother sewing the clothes!

The first old patchwork quilts I saw in the UK were at Claverton Manor in Bath. I loved the geometric shapes, the many different fabrics that appeared in one quilt, the texture of the quilting – I loved it all! I bought a small book about the quilts at the museum and studied the slightly-out-of-focus pictures to see how to go about sewing these quilts. From other books I learned to draft my own blocks and make templates to cut the fabrics from. I then spent many an hour on my sewing machine piecing the tops with fabrics from the scrap bag and then many an evening in front of the television, quilting.

Taking my inspiration from the quilts sewn in years gone by and the wonderful fabrics being produced today, I endeavour to sew quilts and share them with others who also want to sew quilts. When I'm teaching, I often find inspiration from a quilt made in one of my classes. The String Stars and Spiders' Web quilt shown opposite was created after listening to my students.

"I can spend many happy hours pondering all the possibilities that groups of interlocking geometric shapes have to offer."

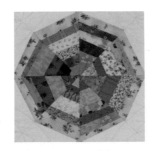

The great thing about this quilt is that it can be created from scraps – or provide you with a wonderful excuse to go out and buy more fabrics!

Carolyn Forster Inspirations

Today, with so many historical documentation schemes and museums recognizing the importance of textiles in history, there is a huge selection of books featuring old quilts. Some of these books go into the family history and daily lives of the maker, which is fascinating to me. I also love looking at books that contain individual patchwork blocks not yet sewn into quilts. I jot down ideas in notebooks of squared paper, and if I am particularly taken with a block and its possibilities then a whole notebook will be given over to that block and all of its variations. I hesitate to call this designing – I think of it along the lines of doodling rather than 'visual note taking'!

At some stage the ideas from the old quilts and blocks, and the fabrics that I have been accumulating, seem to merge together as one being appropriate for the other, and I begin to cut and sew. I think that if the women who made the quilts I see in museums and books could find the scraps and time to sew in their lives, then surely today, with all our modern conveniences, we have no excuse not to sew the odd quilt or two!

What are Strings?

As you start working through this chapter, the first question you might ask is, what are strings? Traditionally, strings were the odd pieces left over from dressmaking. These pieces were often of varying lengths and widths with no uniformity to them. They could however be sewn to a foundation by a thrifty seamstress to form blocks for a quilt made from fabric that would otherwise be discarded.

My students often complain that when they are cutting their pre-washed and pressed fabric, they have to trim off a 'string', a good 1in–2in (2.5cm–5cm), to straighten up the edge before cutting the patches for their quilt project. They then discard this untidy and misshapen strip as it does not appear to be good for anything. Quite rightly, they see this as wastage! Some industrious people do use these strings of fabric for stuffing pincushions, whilst others gather them together to use as ties for plants in their garden – all highly commendable. I, however, see them as the beginnings of more quilts!

Quilts made of these discarded fabric strips are like an album of quilts past. When your eye travels over the entire quilt you pick out different fabrics that went into previous quilts. These quilts may have been given as gifts, put in cupboards ready for the cold weather to set in, or be seasonal quilts that decorate the house as the seasons change, so you don't see them and the fabrics they contain regularly.

Fabric for a string quilt accumulates over time. You won't have enough strings for a quilt as soon as you have finished sewing your current quilt. You need to put the strings from that quilt into a bag. When you next sew a quilt, there will be strips and strings, and these too will go into the bag. With each new project you sew, the strings go in and eventually you will look in the bag and say, 'Oh my goodness – where has all that fabric come from?' Now will be the time to use all that fabric to make a string quilt with all of this 'free' fabric. Don't worry if you can't wait though, cutting strips and strings from your stash is quite acceptable to move the quilt along sooner!

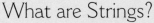

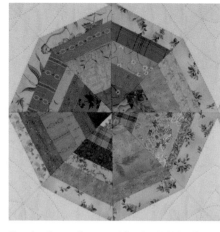

Making String Quilts

There are various ways to sew these quilts but mostly they are made by thoughtless, blissful sewing at your sewing machine or by hand if it suits you better. You will not be concentrating on calculations and the right bit going next to the right bit, or even which colour goes with which. There will be a morning's worth of organizing, which is not arduous as this is all 'free' fabric with no budget to consider, or even whether you have enough of one colour/print, and what will happen if you do run out. This is a quilt where you will make do with what you have, and if you run out you will just use something else. It can be quite liberating – a bit of a patchwork holiday!

Think back to the times when women made these quilts through necessity. They had to use the bits left over. There wasn't a fabric store up the road, or good mail order, or internet shopping. All was not lost though: if there was a monthly trip in the wagon to the big market town, and enough house-keeping was spare, then there could be a glorious time spent in the dry-goods store looking at bolts of fabric to choose one for your borders or sashing depending on the blocks you had sewn. And we can do that too. Because we have virtuously used our 'free' fabric, we can treat ourselves to something new and off the bolt, to border, back or bind the quilt with. And when we get our purchase home and wash and iron it, it will need that misshapen edge trimmed off – and put in the strips-and-strings bag, ready to be in another 'free' quilt, when the time comes!

You may be asking, where will I get strings if I can't wait to start my own string quilt? The answer is, work through your stash, cutting off strips from each fabric, not worrying about consistent width or whether they are straight or not. You will soon accumulate enough for a block or two's worth of sewing. You can also boost your selection by taking advantage of the pre-cut strips that come in 2½in (6.3cm) and 1½in (3.8cm) widths. So grab your strings and let's get quilting!

For the String Stars and Spiders' Webs Quilt described over the next few pages I used a subtle colour palette, which blends nicely with the calico used for the 'stars'. The finished quilt has a warm, antique feel that would suit many types of décor.

This version of the String Stars and Spiders' Webs Quilt uses a much brighter palette of colours, giving the quilt a more contemporary look. Using a pale colour for the 'stars' really makes all the colours sing.

String Stars and Spiders' Webs Quilt

To me, strings and other offcuts of fabric are the beginnings of new quilting projects and this quilt, with its subtle and mellow colours, has the old-fashioned look I love. The quilt is based on a calico foundation, which also forms the 'stars' in the quilt, but you could use other foundation materials – see page 42 for suggestions. The project was designed using imperial measurements and although metric equivalents have been provided, the best results will be obtained using imperial.

Size of finished quilt: 76½in x 76½in (194.3cm x 194.3cm).

Materials

All fabric measurements are based on a workable width of 40in–42in (102cm–107cm) and cutting is always across the width of the fabric unless otherwise stated

- For the strips and strings, a constant colour/print to outline the stars, 30in (80cm) in total, based on needing eleven or twelve strips 1½in–2½in (3.8cm–6.3cm) wide
- For the strips and strings for the spiders' webs, 4yd (3.75m) approximately
- Calico for foundation 3¾yd (3.4m)
- Border fabric 1⅞yd (1.8m)
- Backing fabric, for a backing 82in x 82in (208.3cm x 208.3cm), 4½yd (4.25m) in total
- Binding fabric 20in (51cm) (eight strips 2½in/6.3cm wide and joined in a continuous length)
- Wadding (batting) 82in x 82in (208.3cm x 208.3cm)
- Quilting thread as desired

Making the web blocks

1 Start by cutting sixteen squares from the calico, each 16¼in x 16¼in (41.27cm x 41.27cm). Cut each of these into four quarter-square triangles (Fig 1).

2 Trace template A (given full size on page 43) on to thin card. Position the template on the wrong side of a calico triangle as shown in Fig 2 and mark the shape of the template in pencil – these two lines will be the initial sewing lines.

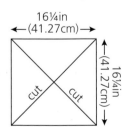

Fig 1

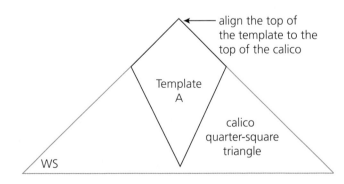

Fig 2

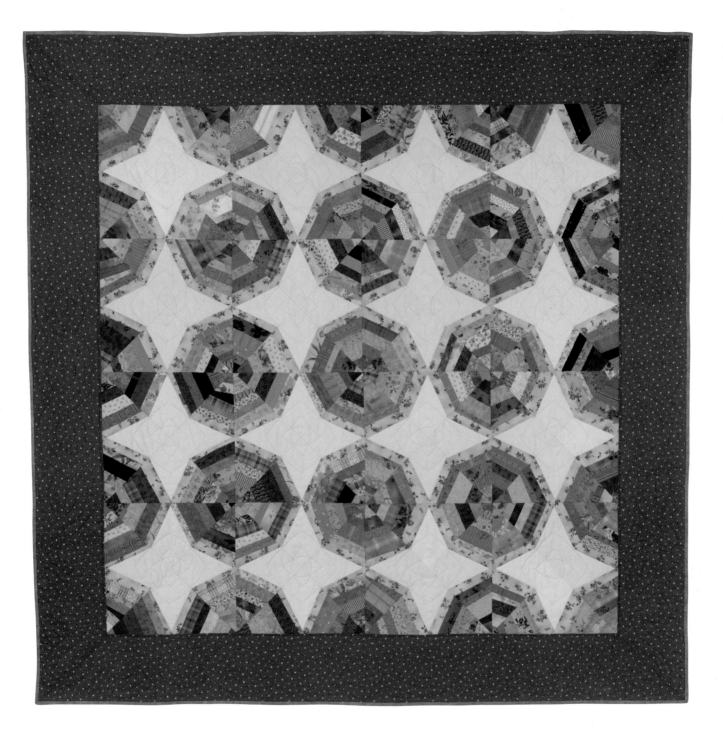

"Making a string quilt is very satisfying. Not only can you can make a charming scrap quilt in the true tradition of patchwork, but the strips used to make the quilt can be offcuts and so will be almost free fabric."

38

3 Flip the calico triangle over and place a strip of fabric on the right side of the triangle so that you can see the 'tails' on either end of the drawn line on the back (Fig 3). The majority of the strip will be towards the template kite shape on the calico, with about ¼in (6mm) on the other side of the line.

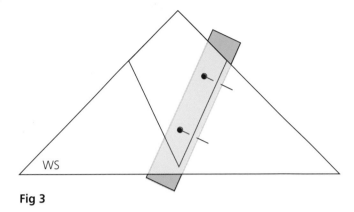

Fig 3

4 Sew along the line (Fig 4). Flip the strip so the right side of the fabric is facing up and finger-press the seam flat (Fig 5).

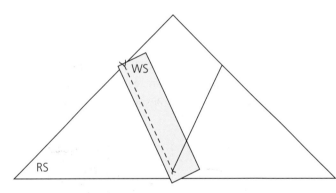

Fig 4

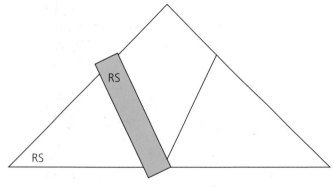

Fig 5

5 Repeat this process along the second line of the template (Fig 6). You are now ready to start sewing from the front of the triangle.

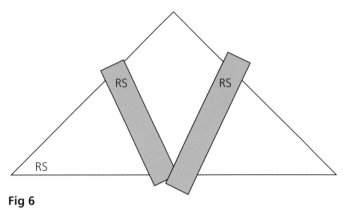

Fig 6

6 Place a fabric strip right sides together with a strip already sewn to the calico and sew together through the calico as well using the same ¼in (6mm) seam (Fig 7). Flip the new strip over to show the right side of the fabric and press (Fig 8).

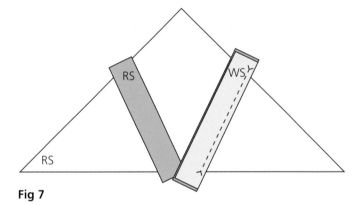

Fig 7

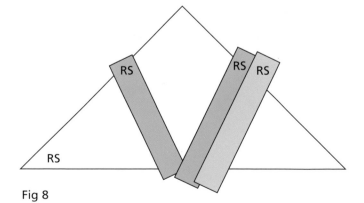

Fig 8

Tip

For quickness you can finger-press seams as you go if you like. The calico foundation will keep the fabrics from stretching.

7 Repeat the process on the other half of the triangle (Fig 9) and continue in this way until the whole wedge of the triangle is covered (Fig 10).

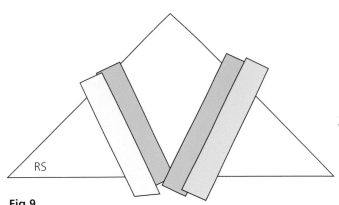

Fig 9

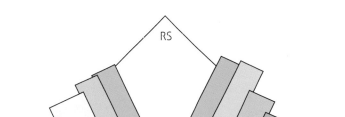

Fig 10

Tip

You might want to use a larger strip towards the corner because any tiny pieces will get lost in the seam allowance and create unnecessary bulk.

8 From the wrong side of the triangle, trim off all the excess ends to create a neat triangle, using the calico foundation as your guide (Fig 11).

WS

trim
trim WS trim

Fig 11

Tip

Once you have understood and practised the process, you can chain piece (see page 108) on the machine and use longer strips of fabric.

9 When you have completed four triangle sections, sew them together to reform a square, as shown in the picture detail below. Press the seams open to avoid bulk where the triangle points meet.

10 Repeat this piecing procedure until all the calico triangles have been sewn into squares. Lay out the blocks in a pleasing manner. Sew the blocks together row by row, pressing all seams open. Now sew the rows together and press seams open.

Tip

If you want to use this as a group quilt or a friendship project, give all the members the same fabric foundation and fabric for the star outline, so it will be the same on all of the blocks, and then let them fill in the spider's web triangles with their own selection of fabrics. When they bring their four triangles back, they can swap three of them with other group members, and then sew them together into a square to be put together in the quilt. This way there is a good distribution of everyone's strings around the quilt. You might prefer to use brighter, more contemporary fabrics for your quilt, as shown below and on page 35.

Adding the border

For a border with mitred corners, measure your quilt top and refer to the instructions on page 111. If you prefer you could add a border with straight (butted) edges – see page 110.

Tip

When mitring corners, it sometimes works well to start sewing from the middle of the border out to the corners, so the fabric doesn't 'shift' towards one end of the seam.

Marking for quilting

1 Layer the quilt top with the wadding (batting) and the backing fabric and tack (baste) together (see page 112).

2 I quilted this piece 'in the ditch' around all of the stars (see page 112 for further information on quilting). After this, I marked the pattern in the stars using templates C and D on page 44, rotating template C 90 degrees to achieve the crossed shape. The strings in the spiders' webs were quilted through the centre of random strings. The border was then quilted ¼in (6mm) away from the edge.

Tip

Use a bodkin or a hera marker to 'score' the quilting design onto the quilt. Because it is a non-invasive method, like chalk or soap slivers, you do not need to worry about removing it when the quilting is done.

4 Now mirror image the design and mark it on the other side of the mitre (Fig 13). Before continuing along the next side of the border draw the ellipse in the centre of that side and work *back* towards the corner. This way if the shapes are not matching up you can elongate or contract an ellipse to fit, whilst still getting all of the corners symmetrical and exactly the same on all four corners.

3 The quilting in the border follows a 'ric-rac' cable pattern, using template E on page 45. Draw the cable so that it fits around the corners, as follows. Start by drawing the first ellipse in the centre of one side of the border (Fig 12a). Draw another ellipse, interlocking with the first as shown in Fig 12b. Continue to create the cable in this way until you reach the mitred corner (Fig 12c).

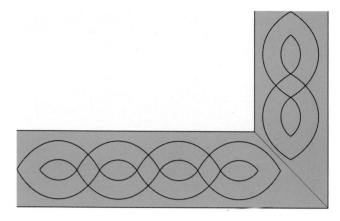

Fig 13

5 Use the template horizontally to mark the shape across the corner mitre but stopping on the mitre line, as in Figs 14a and 14b. Turn the template 90 degrees and mark the shape vertically, as in Fig 14c. Fig 14d shows the finished corner.

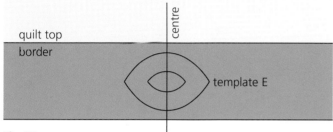

Fig 12a

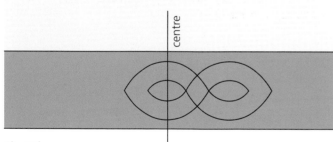

Fig 12b

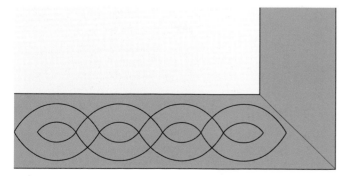

Fig 12c

Fig 14a

Fig 14b

Fig 14c

Fig 14d

6 Now continue marking the ellipse template across the border, as you did in step 4 previously. If you end up with a gap between one ellipse and the centre one marked previously, it is at this point that you may have to elongate or contract an ellipse slightly to fit.

7 Mark the other two sides of the border in the same way. Using chalk, fill in more boldly the lines that you want to quilt to create the ric-rac effect (Fig 15). The border is now ready for quilting by hand or machine.

Fig 15

Finishing the quilt

When the quilt is completely quilted, trim off the surplus backing and wadding and apply the binding – see page 114 for instructions. If you want a double-fold binding, to make 320in (813cm) of binding, cut eight strips 2½in (6.3cm) wide and join into a continuous length. Fold wrong sides together and then press.

Making the quilt without a calico foundation

If you do not want to use calico as a foundation and therefore as the 'stars' in the quilt, try one of these other methods as the foundation. Some foundations, like the calico, can be left in place, whilst others will need to be removed before layering the quilt together.

Using paper

Use newspaper or old telephone directory pages. Cut into triangles as you would the calico. From fabric for the star (allow about 1m/1yd) cut template B (see opposite), position on the paper and pin in place or use repositionable spray adhesive. Place the first string right sides together, match up the raw edges of the fabrics and sew through the fabrics and the paper. Continue until the paper is completely covered. Neaten the triangle and carefully tear away the paper. Use spray starch if the fabric needs stabilizing.

Tip

If using paper or newspaper as a foundation, set your sewing machine on a slightly smaller stitch than usual so that it is easier to tear the paper away afterwards.

Using Vilene

You can use lightweight, sew-in Vilene as a foundation in the same way as newspaper but it can be left in place.

Using foundation sheets

I use EQ foundation sheets, which are a non-woven, rayon/polyester blend. The material, which is perfect for foundation piecing, is easy to see through and sew on, won't dull needles and can be torn away or be left in place if need be. Use as you would newspaper.

Using wash-away foundation paper

These can be used in the same way as newspaper, but will dissolve in water instead of being torn away.

"There, your string quilt is finished. Keep your 'string bag' well filled and you will soon have enough for another lovely quilt."

String Stars and Spiders' Webs –
templates and quilting patterns

All templates are full size

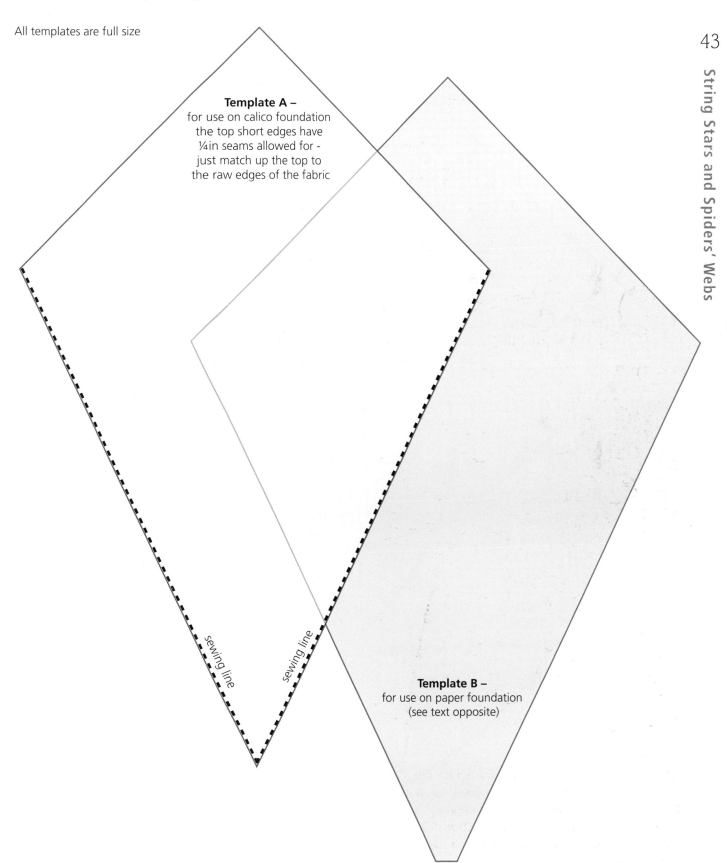

Template A –
for use on calico foundation
the top short edges have
¼in seams allowed for -
just match up the top to
the raw edges of the fabric

sewing line

sewing line

Template B –
for use on paper foundation
(see text opposite)

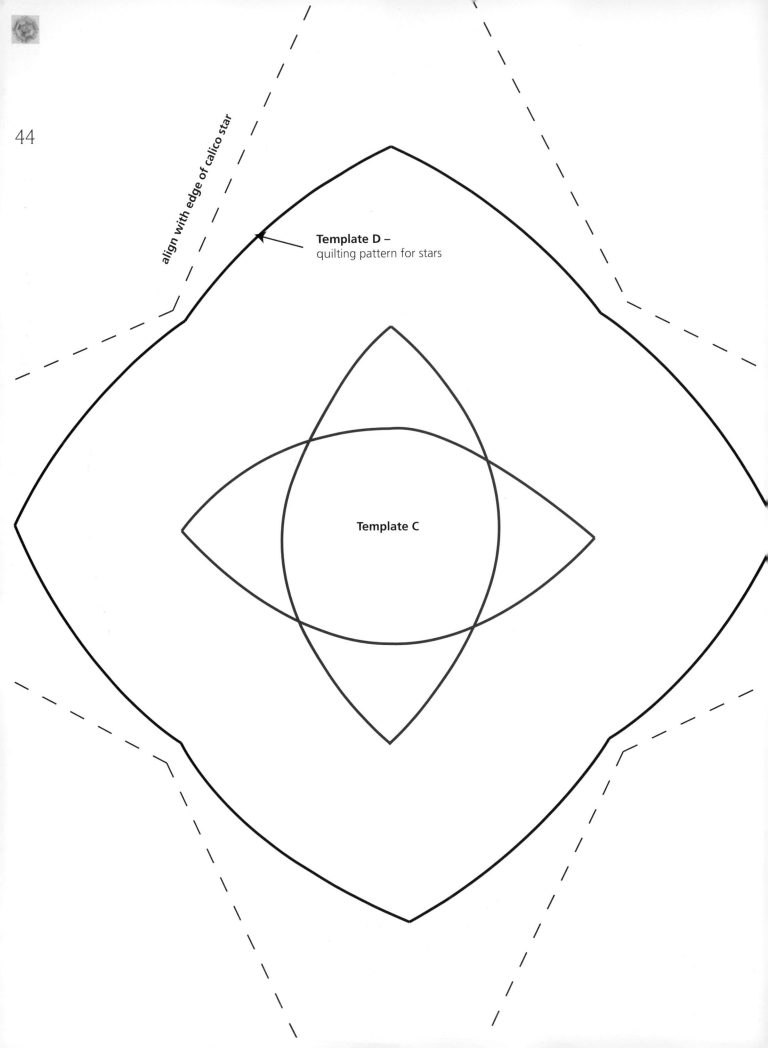

44

align with edge of calico star

Template D –
quilting pattern for stars

Template C

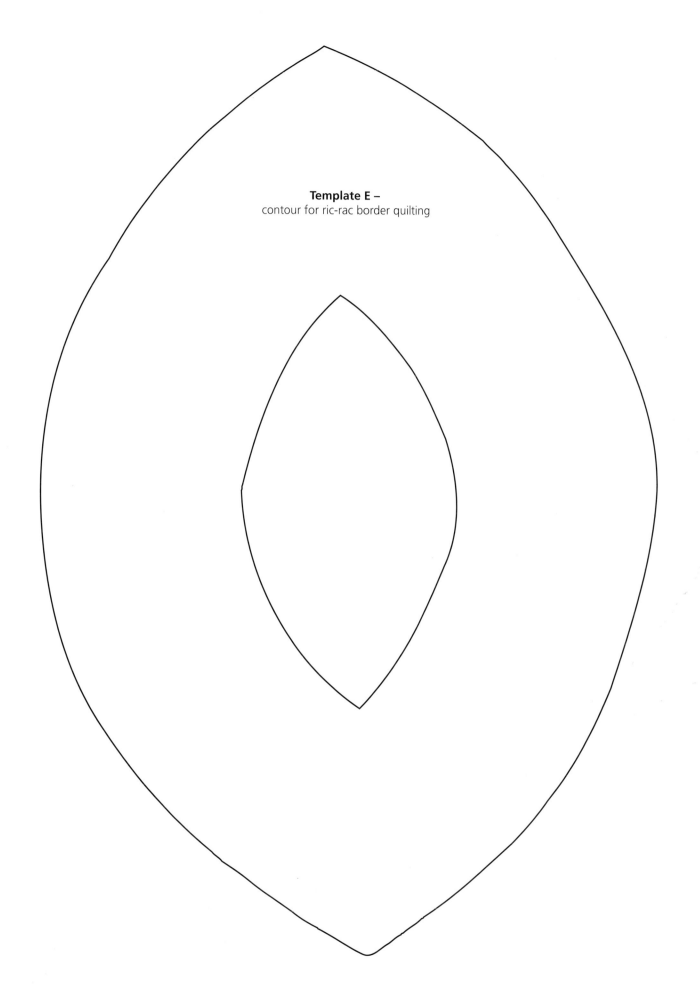

Template E –
contour for ric-rac border quilting

Country-Style Welcome
by Lynette Anderson-O'Rourke, Australia

My love of patchwork and quilting really began in 1981 when I decided I needed a hobby that was portable and easy to pick up and put down. So I took a night class and over ten weeks made a hand-stitched traditional sampler quilt and by the end of the course I was totally addicted! In 1984 my family moved to the Channel Islands, UK, and I started teaching patchwork from home as there was no island quilt store. I also sold my handmade pillows and small quilts at the local craft centre. Six years later we moved to Australia and my patchwork designs blossomed.

The inspiration for my designs comes from so many parts of my life – a memory from childhood, where I grew up in a small village in Dorset, England, or from something occurring in my daily life in Australia today. I find inspiration at every turn of my head: sometimes the ideas come tumbling out in a jumble and at other times my mind is blank and I wonder if I will ever manage to produce anything again! But give me a pencil and paper and I am one happy girl. Of course that then leads to needing fabrics, needle and threads. The end result could be a simple design for a pillow or a wonderful quilt design.

Over the years I have learnt that whilst the ideas are flowing I need to get them on to paper, maybe even stitch a little so I can see how it's going to work and what colours I may like to use. I then move to the next idea. When the time comes for me to stitch something new I review and refine my earlier drawings and have fun selecting the fabrics and threads ready for the best part, the stitching.

"Traditionally samplers were embroidered, to teach children a variety of stitches. This welcome sampler is no different other than it is made in patchwork rather than embroidery."

Take the humble pineapple, international symbol of welcome, and combine it with a simple house, trees and flowers, throw in some letters and numbers and you have the makings of a charming sampler.

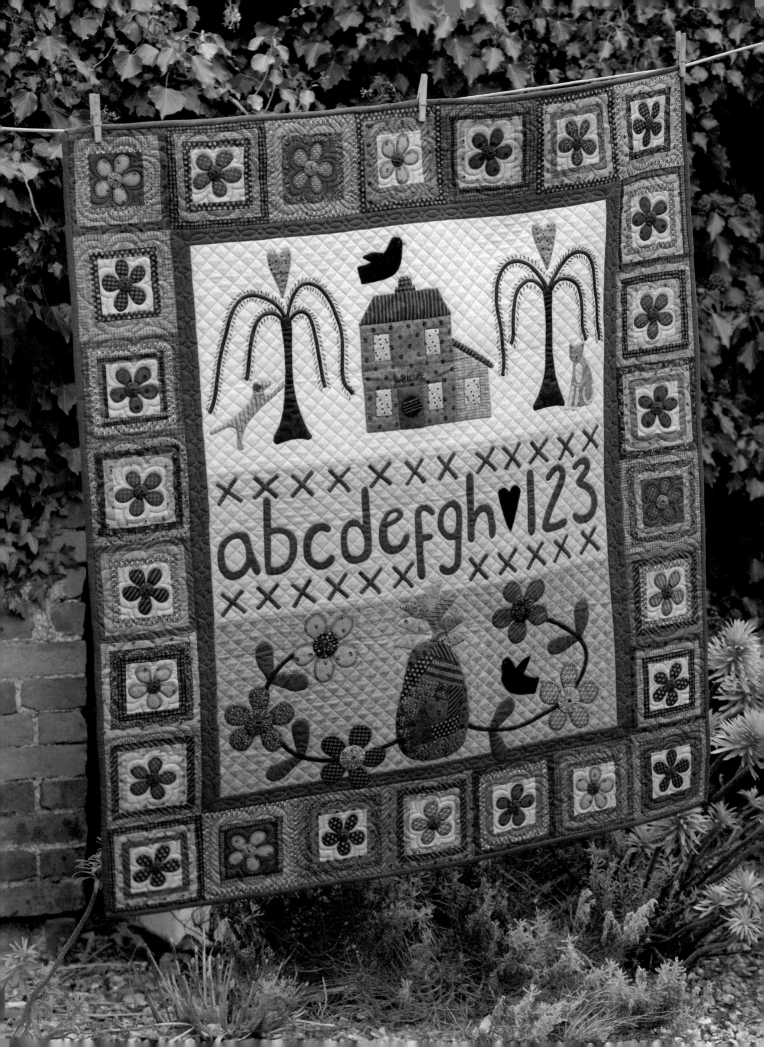

Lynette Anderson-O'Rourke Inspirations

I started designing and producing my own patterns under the label 'Lynette Anderson for The Patchwork Angel' in 1995, five years after we moved to Australia. The name angel was chosen as my Dad always called my brother and I his angels! I was very fortunate as my patterns were popular immediately, and some of those early patterns are as popular today as they have ever been. In 1997, with the help of my Mum, we opened a quilt store, which we called The Patchwork Angel. We had the store for almost ten wonderful, busy years but eventually I decided it was time to focus full time on my designing and we sold the store. These days I live by the beach and work from a studio at home. I am very lucky as all four of my boys and my parents live here on Queensland's Sunshine Coast, so we get to spend lots of time together, which of course gives me lots of inspiration!

As well as my patchwork and quilting designs, I also work for Henry Glass & Co producing my own fabric lines. The whole process has been a wonderful experience, from posting off my little paintings, seeing how their design team interprets them and finally the excitement of working with my own fabrics (see page 117 for more information).

Patchwork is a very large part of my daily life and each day is an adventure. The feel and smell of fabric is unique and it brings me great joy every time I work with it. First comes the drawing and planning of a project then the choosing of the fabrics and threads. The colours and patterns on the fabrics you use play an important role in the finished look of your quilt, so take your time and enjoy choosing your fabrics. Then comes the cutting and shaping of the pieces, the rhythm of the stitching, the dreaming you can do whilst working and of course the simple pleasure of creating something beautiful.

Much of my inspiration comes from my everyday life. In this patchwork piece Hugo the dog is watching Nora's horses from the other side of the fence. The new foal is at his mother's feet relaxing in the quiet of a spring morning. The addition of the beautiful hand-painted dog button set this stitchery off perfectly. I have made mine into a simple pillow but you could frame the stitchery or use it as a pocket on a bag. There are three patterns in this series — to see Nora's Hens, and Nora's Garden — see page 118 for website details.

Impress everyone with this gorgeous 'Here Kitty' sewing accessory collection. With its seriously cute tote bag, matching needlecase, tape measure cover and scissor holder….what more could a girl want — well, maybe a diamond ring but hey, that's not a sewing accessory, or is it?

In this patchwork, Your Home or Mine, there are castles, cottages and a gypsy caravan. I designed twelve different home blocks each one a combination of appliqué and stitchery, effectively bordered by English paper-pieced triangles. The joining blocks are simply nine-patch and one-patch blocks resulting in a stunning quilt. The Butterfly Collection (folded) uses reproduction fabrics and was inspired by the era when butterflies were collected and framed. A Bee's Life Bag and the Saltbox Sampler pillow feature gorgeous hand-painted buttons and simple stitchery.

These pincushions appeared in my first self-published book *The Pincushion Book* in 1998. The book has long been out of print but the popularity of the pincushions still thrives, so I have released some of the designs as patterns.

These pieces are from a nine month block-of-the-month quilt called A Kitten's Tale. The designs were inspired by our family pets, Hugo the dog and the cats Fatcat, Freckle and Felix, and the crazy antics they get up to daily. This quilt was a delight to design and stitch with its combination of appliqué, simple piecing, stitchery and the fabulously fun yoyos.

Welcome Sampler

This sampler includes a variety of techniques, such as traditional piecing and appliqué, blanket stitch appliqué, bias strips for stems, yoyos and a small amount of embroidery. I wanted to create a scrap-bag look for this quilt, as if I had pulled leftover fabrics from my dressmaking scrap bag. To get this effect I have used about thirty assorted small-print fabrics and tried to use them randomly throughout the quilt. The various parts are made separately and then the whole quilt is assembled in panels, with borders added. The project was designed using imperial measurements and although metric equivalents have been provided the quilt works best using imperial.

Size of finished quilt: 45½in x 52in (115cm x 132cm).

Materials

Fabric amounts are across the width of the fabric unless otherwise stated

- Light cream fabric for background 18in (45cm)
- Mid cream fabric for background and log cabin centres 24in (60cm)
- Caramel fabric for background 18in (45cm)
- Dark green fabric 18in (45cm) for inner border, letters, leaves and centres for log cabins
- Fat eighths of about thirty assorted small-print fabrics, for appliqué and log cabin strips
- One fat quarter of dark brown fabric for tree trunks, branches and vine
- Black wool 6in (15cm) square for crows and heart
- Double-sided fusible webbing (such as Vliesofix)
- Lightweight interfacing (such as Vilene) for crazy-patch pineapple foundation
- DMC stranded cotton (floss): 782 old gold, 838 dark brown, 931 blue, 936 dark green and 310 black
- Genziana wool/acrylic thread: 329 black and 468 dark green (or alternatively use six strands of DMC stranded cotton)
- Basting glue (optional) (I used Roxanne's Glue Baste It ™)
- Fine-tipped fabric marking pen
- Bias press bar ¼in (6mm) (optional)
- Template plastic
- One large button for front door
- Wadding (batting) 50in x 55in (127cm x 140cm) approx
- Backing fabric 50in x 55in (127cm x 140cm) approx
- Binding fabric 200in x 2½in (508cm x 6.3cm) approx
- Quilting threads as desired

Making the bias stems

1 Begin your quilt by making the bias stems. These are made from fabric strips cut on the cross grain (bias) direction of the fabric (see diagram in Tip overleaf). Cutting bias strips makes the fabric more flexible and easier to shape. There are various ways to make bias stems but I prefer to use bias press bars. These allow you to press a tube of fabric flat, ready to stitch into place.

2 Use the dark brown fat quarter to make approximately 3m (3yd) of ¼in (6mm) wide bias. This does not need to be in one length. Take the fat quarter and fold it in half diagonally (see Fig 1a and 1b below). Open out the fabric and cut the strips on the bias (cross-grain) to the desired width (Fig 1c).

fat quarter of fabric

Fig 1a

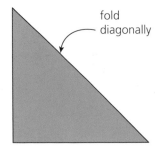

fold diagonally

Fig 1b

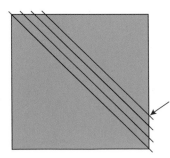

open out and then cut strips on cross grain in the desired width

Fig 1c

"The inspiration for this quilt came while I was out to lunch with a friend and saw a wonderful display of pineapples in a café. I came home and researched the fruit and discovered their wonderful symbolic meaning – and my design grew from there."

3 Fold the bias strip in half lengthwise, with wrong sides together. Using a ¼in (6mm) seam, stitch along the raw edges of the folded strip. Trim away any excess seam allowance, as this will make the finished bias stem less bulky.

4 If using a bias bar, insert the bias bar of the appropriate size into the stem. Twist the seam to the back of the bias bar and press with a hot iron. Slip the bias bar along the length of the stem turning the seam to the back and pressing as you go. If your fabric has a tendency to lose the press try using a light spray of starch.

If you are not using a bias bar, place the tube of fabric on the ironing board, seam up and central. Iron along the length of the tube, flattening it and making sure the seam stays in the centre down the fabric length. Place the bias stems aside for later use.

Making the yoyos

1 Yoyos are sometimes known as Suffolk Puffs. There are two sizes of yoyos needed for this quilt, used for the centres of the flowers – five of the large size and twenty-six of the small size (see pictures above). Make both sizes using the full-size templates on page 56, tracing the shapes on to template plastic.

2 Using a fine-tipped fabric marking pen, draw around the template on the wrong side of your fabrics. Cut out on the line (the seam allowance has been included in the template).

3 Thread your needle with a double strand of sewing cotton and knot one end. Take one of the circles you've cut and with the wrong side facing fold over approximately ¼in (6mm). Make a running stitch around the entire edge (see Fig 3a), turning the ¼in (6mm) in as you go and gathering it slightly.

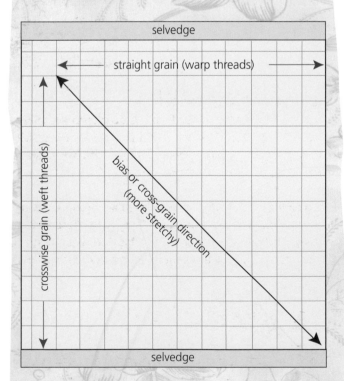

Tip

The bias or cross-grain direction of a piece of woven fabric is at 45 degrees to its warp and weft threads (see Fig 2 below). Fabric is more elastic in this direction. To calculate the width of fabric to cut for your stems, double the finished width of the stem and add ½in (1.3cm) for seams and ⅛in (3mm) for ease.

selvedge

straight grain (warp threads)

crosswise grain (weft threads)

bias or cross-grain direction
(more stretchy)

selvedge

Fig 2 Fabric grain

Tip

When making a yoyo try to keep your running stitches about ¼in (6mm) in length as this will give a nice sized opening in the centre of your yoyo.

4 Once you have got back to where you started, gently pull on the thread to gather it – you may need to wriggle the yoyo between your fingers to get it into shape (Fig 3b). Pull the thread firmly once you are happy with the look of your yoyo and then end the thread off at the back. Flatten the yoyo slightly.

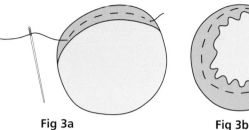
Fig 3a

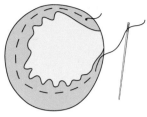
Fig 3b

Making the crazy-patch pineapple

1 Using the pineapple template on page 59 make the template from template plastic. Take a piece of lightweight interfacing and mark the pineapple shape on to it using a fine-tipped fabric pen. Cut out the shape but add a generous ½in (1.3cm) seam allowance.

2 Beginning with a five-sided piece of fabric, place the fabric in the centre of the foundation interfacing, right side up, and pin in position (Fig 4a). Take another fabric strip, place it right sides together on one edge of the first piece and machine or hand stitch it in place (Fig 4b). Finger-press open (Fig 4c).

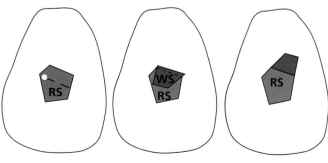
Fig 4a   **Fig 4b**   **Fig 4c**

3 Working clockwise continue adding strips, randomly selecting the fabrics as you go (Fig 4d). Remember to press open after each addition. Continue adding fabric pieces until the whole foundation is covered (Fig 4e). Press well.

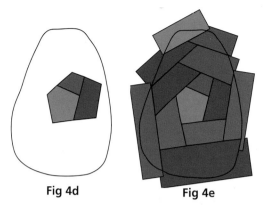
Fig 4d   **Fig 4e**

4 On the wrong side of the foundation re-mark the pineapple shape and cut to shape leaving a generous ¼in (6mm) seam allowance. Clip seams on concave curves (the curves that go inwards). Tack (baste) under the ¼in (6mm) seam allowance and press well. The pineapple leaves will be appliquéd in place later. Place the pineapple aside for the moment.

Making the top panel

1 From light cream background fabric cut one rectangle 15½in high x 30½in wide (39.4cm x 77.5cm). Fold the fabric in half widthways and gently finger-press the centre. This will enable you to centre the house on the background.

2 Using the picture above or on page 51 as a guide and using your favourite method of appliqué, apply the house, roof, chimney, windows, front door, cat and dog. See page 110 for instructions on appliqué and page 109 for reversing templates.

Tip

When using traditional appliqué, I use a basting glue to fix the shapes in position on the background. Roxanne's Glue Baste It has a small tube through which tiny drops of glue emerge, allowing for fine placement of the glue. You could use pins but I don't like the way the thread gets caught around the pins when I'm sewing the shapes into place.

3 Position the tree trunks and then take some of the bias you made previously and using the picture as a guide cut some lengths of the bias and tuck the ends into the top of the tree trunk, arranging the branches nicely (see Fig 5a below). Once you are happy with the positions you can either pin them in place or use basting glue. Stitch the branches in place making sure the ends of the branches are turned under at the ends.

4 With a fine-tipped fabric marking pen mark the leaves on the background fabric alongside the branches (see Fig 5b). Stitch the leaves in long stitch using two strands of Genziana thread 468 dark green (or use six strands of dark green 936 DMC stranded cotton). Position the hearts at the top of the trees and appliqué them in place.

Fig 5a

tuck the ends of the bias branches into the top of the tree

Fig 5b

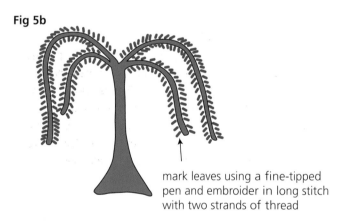

mark leaves using a fine-tipped pen and embroider in long stitch with two strands of thread

5 I stitched the crow in place using Genziana wool/acrylic thread colour 329 black (or use six strands of black 310 DMC stranded cotton). The crow's eye, beak and feet were stitched using two strands of DMC 782 old gold. The dog's collar was stitched in satin stitch using two strands of DMC 931 blue.

Tip
Cutting the crow from wool means that the edges do not need turning under. You could also use felt in a similar way.

Making the middle panel

1 From mid cream background fabric cut a rectangle 10½in high x 30½in wide (26.7cm x 77.5cm). Using the picture as a guide for positioning and your favourite method of appliqué, apply the Xs, the letters, the numbers and the heart. I used traditional appliqué for the Xs and fusible web appliqué with blanket stitch for the letters and numbers.

2 The heart was cut from wool so the edges don't need turning under. I stitched the heart into place using Genziana wool/acrylic thread colour 329 black.

Making the bottom panel

1 From caramel background fabric cut one rectangle 12½in high x 30½in wide (31.75cm x 77.5cm). Fold the fabric in half widthways and finger-press the centre line – this will enable you to centre the crazy-patch pineapple that you made earlier.

2 Pin or baste glue the pineapple into position. Use the large flower template on page 59 to make five flower shapes. Using the picture as a guide for positioning and your favourite method of appliqué, pin or glue the bias vine, leaves and large flowers into place. Once happy with the positions you can stitch everything. I used the traditional method of appliqué for the pineapple, the pineapple leaves and the leaves on the flower vine. The flowers were attached using the fusible web method of appliqué. Stitch a large yoyo to the centre of each flower.

3 The crow was cut from wool so no edges need to be turned under. I stitched the crow into place using Genziana wool/ acrylic thread colour 329 black. The crow's eye, beak and feet were stitched using two strands of DMC 782 old gold.

Joining the panels

1 Using ¼in (6mm) seams, join the three panels together to form the large centre panel. Press seams open.

2 The inner border can now be added to the centre panel. From dark green fabric cut two strips 1½in x 30½in (3.8cm x 77.5cm) for the top and bottom and cut two strips 1¾in x 39½in (4.5cm x 100.3cm) for the sides (see Tip below). Using a ¼in (6mm) seam join the top and bottom borders to the centre panel and then press seams. Repeat for the side borders.

Tip

Before adding the inner or outer borders, it is a good idea to measure your quilt first, to make sure the measurements given in the project will fit your quilt.

Making the outer border blocks

1 From mid cream fabric cut twenty-two 4in squares and from dark green fabric cut four 4in squares (these measurements include seam allowance). From the assorted thirty coordinating fabrics cut some 1in strips. Using the same fabric for each round, add the strips to the centre square log-cabin style (see Fig 6a–e). Add three rounds of strips to each centre square. The finished size of the log cabin blocks should be 7in (17.8cm), including seam allowance. Press well.

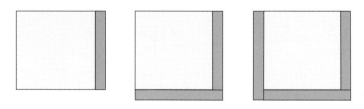

Fig 6a   **Fig 6b**   **Fig 6c**

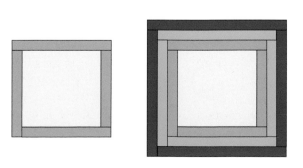

Fig 6d   **Fig 6e**

2 Use the small flower template on page 59 to make twenty-six flowers. Appliqué a small flower to the centre of each block. I used fusible web appliqué and DMC 838 for the blanket stitch. Stitch a small yoyo to the centre of each flower.

3 Choosing six of the border blocks, join them together to form a row 7in x 39½in (17.8cm x 100.3cm), including seam allowance. Using ¼in (6mm) seams, join to one side of the centre panel. Repeat for the other side.

4 Now, choosing seven of the border blocks, join them together to form a row 7in x 46in (17.8cm x 116.8cm), including seam allowance. Using a ¼in (6mm) seams, join to the top of the centre panel. Repeat for the bottom and then press.

Finishing the quilt

Using your preferred method of quilting (see page 112), prepare the quilt sandwich and quilt your quilt. I used a professional machine quilter for my Welcome Sampler. The centre panels are quilted with a background grid pattern. The flower motifs in the outer border are outlined with quilting. Using your preferred method, bind your quilt (see page 114). Label the quilt (see page 114) and lastly, stitch a large old button on the front door.

Tip

I used backstitch and two strands of black DMC stranded cotton to stitch the word 'Welcome' above the door on the house but this is optional or could be changed to a word and language of your choice.

"I hope that this Welcome Sampler brings as much pleasure to you whilst you create yours as it did to me."

56

Country-Style Welcome

Welcome Quilt templates

The templates on these two pages and page 59 are full size; the letters and numbers on page 58 will need enlarging on a photocopier. If using traditional appliqué (see page 110) use the templates as they appear here but add a ¼in (6mm) seam allowance all round. If using fusible web appliqué (see page 110), the templates will need to be reversed – see page 109 for advice on how to do this.

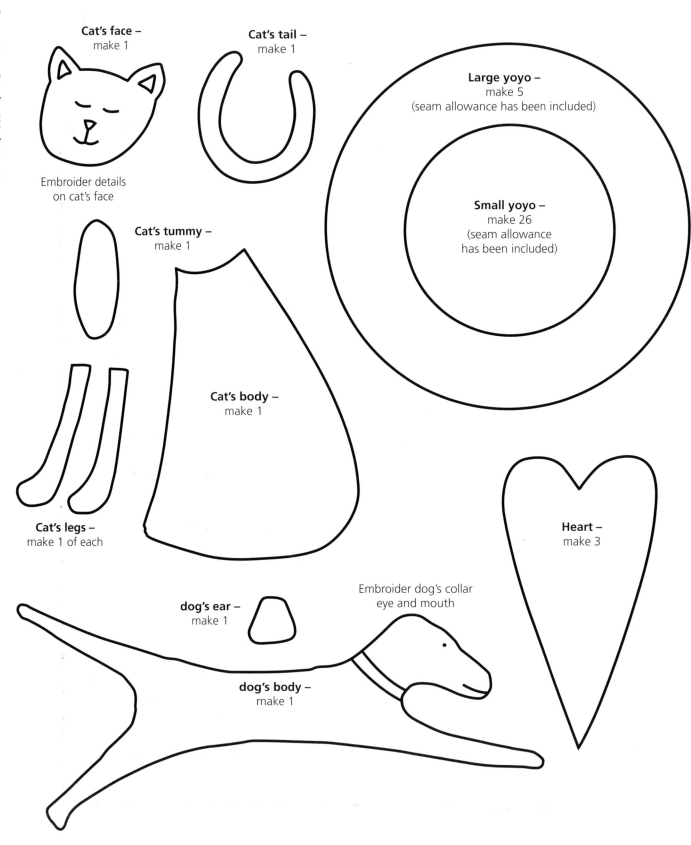

Cat's face – make 1

Embroider details on cat's face

Cat's tail – make 1

Large yoyo – make 5 (seam allowance has been included)

Small yoyo – make 26 (seam allowance has been included)

Cat's tummy – make 1

Cat's body – make 1

Cat's legs – make 1 of each

Heart – make 3

Embroider dog's collar eye and mouth

dog's ear – make 1

dog's body – make 1

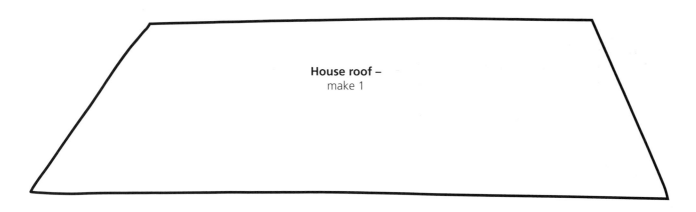

House roof –
make 1

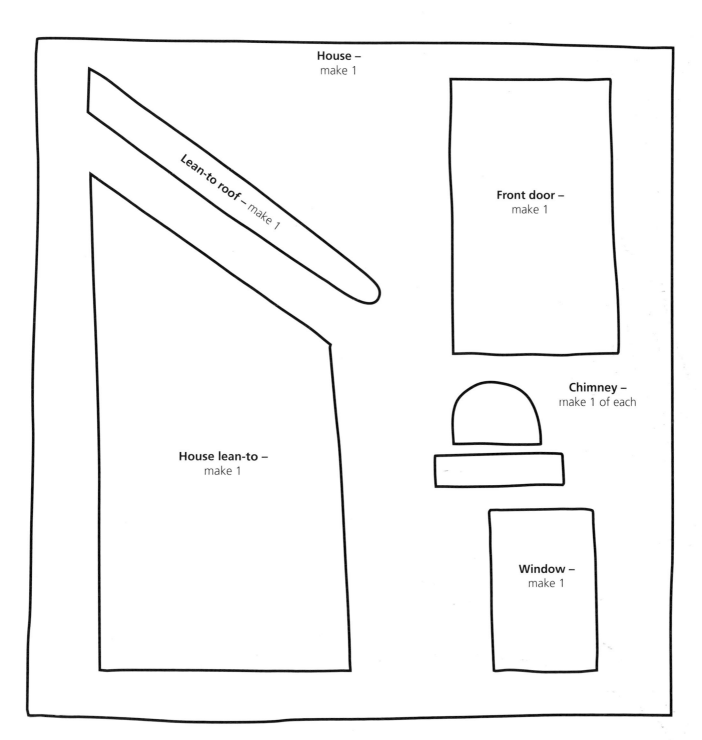

House –
make 1

Lean-to roof – make 1

Front door –
make 1

Chimney –
make 1 of each

House lean-to –
make 1

Window –
make 1

Please note: the letter and number templates on this page are shown at 75% of original size. Enlarge by 134% to trace at full size.

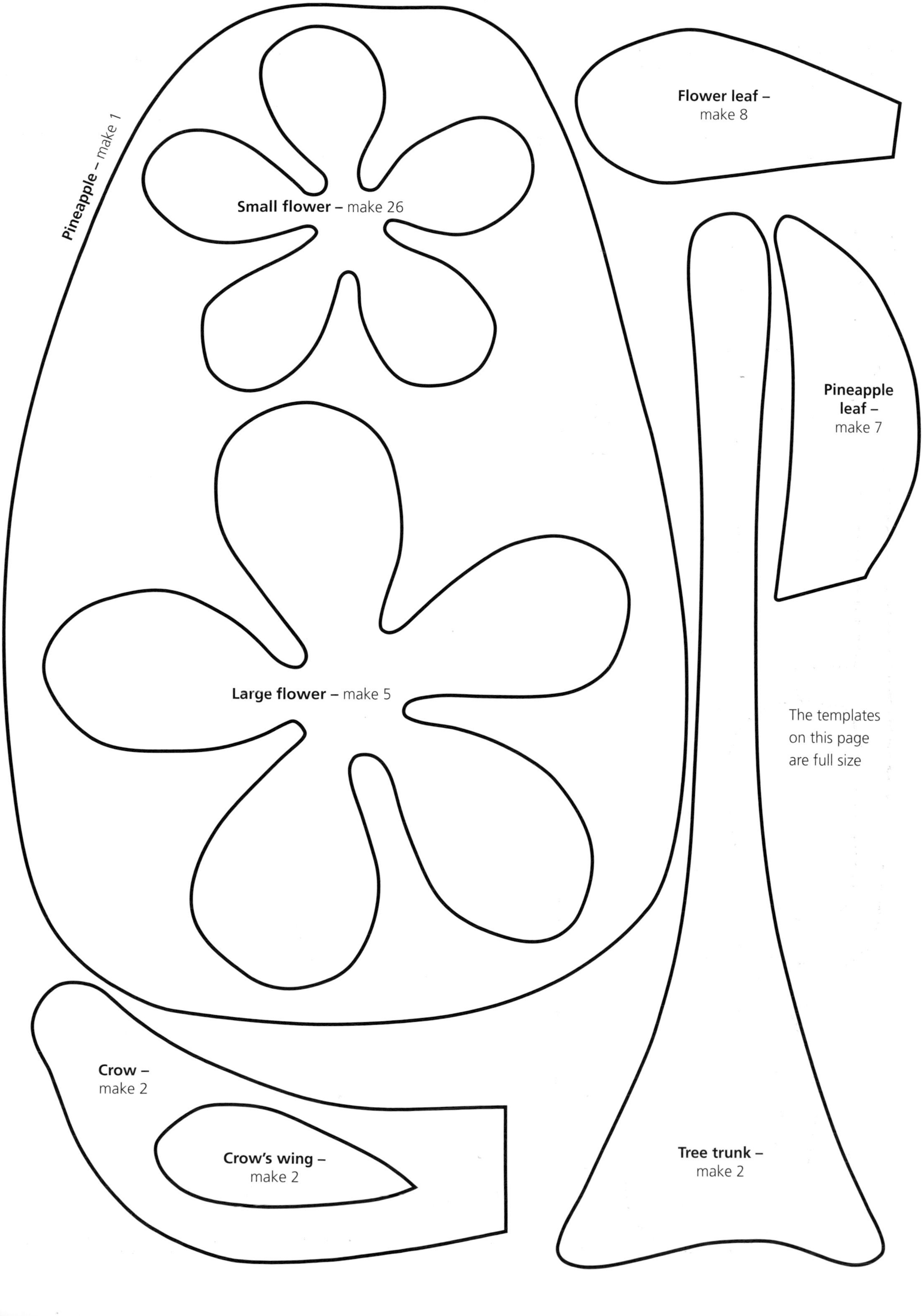

Pineapple – make 1

Small flower – make 26

Large flower – make 5

Crow – make 2

Crow's wing – make 2

Flower leaf – make 8

Pineapple leaf – make 7

The templates on this page are full size

Tree trunk – make 2

Patchwork in Perspective
by Lynne Edwards, UK

I first met up with the concept of perspective as applied to patchwork when I went on a workshop some years ago in Houston, Texas, given by the American quiltmaker and artist Katie Pasquini Masopust. The class was just drafting (technical drawing), with no reference to cutting or stitching fabric, but I found it fascinating. I sat next to a Texan lady called Kay Bruce and as we chatted we discovered a mutual quilting friend in England and there began a friendship that continues to this day.

The following year when I stayed with Kay she showed me a way she had devised of piecing by hand or machine using shapes cut from freezer paper instead of templates. Each freezer paper shape was ironed onto the back of the chosen fabric which was then cut ¼in (6mm) beyond the freezer paper on all sides to give the seam allowances. This was about 15 years ago, remember, when such techniques were unheard of! It is typical of quilters that having thought something out, they immediately share it with fellow quilters, who in their turn, use it, refine or develop it, and show it to others.

Since then I have used this freezer paper piecing method in designs that appear in several of my books and find it invaluable. It provides a choice of technique when piecing, especially for those who find foundation piecing difficult or wasteful of fabric. Its great advantage for me is in being able to position the freezer paper exactly where I want on the fabric so that stripes or specific details on the fabric can be used in the design. What you see is exactly what you get in the final arrangement, which means that creating the design shown opposite is easy – see overleaf for more examples.

"Fear not, although this project is based on sound drafting principles it is not hard sums and anxiety. The maths is already worked out for you, so start choosing fabrics!"

This design, called Perspective Stars, was made by one of my students, Kate Badrick. It uses freezer paper to cut out the shapes required. The project instructions tell you how to make a smaller version of the design (see picture on page 65). See page 74 for advice on making this larger version shown here.

Lynne Edwards Inspirations

There are so many examples of block designs and patterns to be seen in floors, walls and ceilings in ancient buildings that it seemed an exciting concept to imagine a room where every wall, floor and ceiling, would be filled with one simple patchwork block, such as the Ohio Star block shown in Fig 1a on page 64. Each surface when seen face on would be the block without distortion. Standing at one end of the room, only the far wall would show the classic block – the others would show the design narrowing into the distance in perspective as Fig 1b. Looking at it, we know that the distortion is a purely visual phenomenon and that if we walked into the room and stood facing any of those other walls, they would also be true Ohio Star blocks.

An artist struggles to interpret the principles of perspective when trying to capture a landscape in a drawing as they know that without it the interpretation will lack depth and realism. Quilters making traditional geometric blocks have a far easier task as all the measurements are prescribed and regular. By following a set of formal procedures we can distort the block with true perspective and get a stunning effect. Each piece that in the original block was a square or regular triangle becomes a strange shape, unrecognisable when compared with its fellow in the classic block. It is no more difficult to piece than the original block – just different! Here I show you a few more ideas to inspire you.

This darker design places brown stars with swirly batik centres on a lighter textured background. A blue/green version is shown on page 65. Both designs use slightly darker fabric as the background to the centre star to emphasize the perspective effect.

This block is very similar to the Ohio Star but creates a different effect when drawn as a perspective block design. The block can be treated in the same way as the Ohio Star used in the project.

This is a section of a quilt design that I am working on, taking the tiled floor concept a step further. The square tiles that narrow into the distance in true perspective have a secondary design on them made by changing the colours of the tiles and by piecing points in the front centre pair of tiles. I think I am going to make four sides like this around a centre unit, but I'm not too sure yet… See page 75 for advice on how to create a tiled effect.

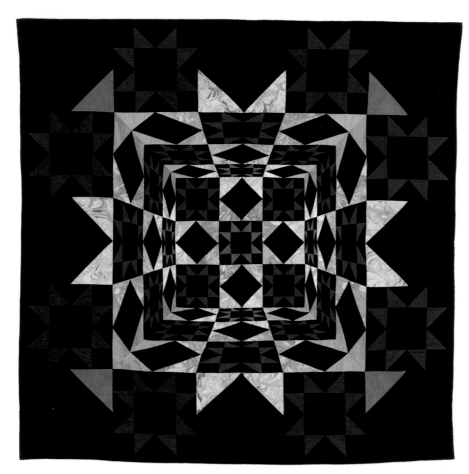

This large wall hanging, called 'Boxed Stars', has a centre design of nine small blocks, Ohio Star alternating with the square-in-a-square design. These same blocks are repeated on each side of the centre in perspective. The more complex design gives more scope for a real three-dimensional effect, especially with the final border of blocks set flat, without perspective, as if they are the front wall opening into the starry room. I'm quite proud of the effect I achieved with this piece. Some viewers actually find it unsettling, as it gives them slight vertigo. My family call it, 'I have fallen down the lift shaft'…

Drafting Equipment

I enjoy measuring, drawing accurately and making calculations, but I am very aware that this is an area that many quilters find intimidating. It is my job as a quilt teacher to try to make every stage of a technique as accessible as possible, which here means a practical approach to mathematics rather than a theoretical one. I will explain the logic behind each stage of the drafting so that those who want to move on to make their own perspective designs know just how to go about it. If you just want to create the project without understanding the mathematical principles underlying it (a bit like the way I am with electricity: plug it in and it works, that's all I need to know…), simply follow the step-by-step instructions for drawing (beginning overleaf) and you'll be fine.

Choosing the Fabric

The design used for the Ohio Star project uses just three fabrics – one for the star centre, one for the star points and a third for the background. Because the aim of the design is to show the amazing three-dimensional effect of true perspective, the fabric should reflect this. For the best effect there needs to be plenty of contrast between star and background, so first choose two allied fabrics for the star and then place them on a possible background fabric to see how they work together. For the background try both light and dark fabrics – you never know what is going to look good until you try arranging them together like this.

Perspective Stars Quilt

The stunning effect of this quilt is created by distorting the Ohio Star block using perspective and results in an intriguing design – see Fig 1a below for the individual Ohio Star block and Fig 1b for the complete layout. This blue/green version of the perspective block uses a really interesting marbled fabric as the star centres and 'floats' the stars on a paler flowery batik – see page 62 for a darker version. The block design is most effective as a small wall hanging but could be made into a cushion. If you wish, the design can be extended to create the larger quilt shown on the page 61 – see page 74 for additional advice. The project was designed using imperial measurements and although metric equivalents have been provided, the best results will be obtained using imperial.

Materials

- Graph paper, preferably marked in inches, at least 16in x 16in (40.6cm x 40.6cm)
- Freezer paper at least 18in x 18in (45.7cm x 45.7cm)
- Paper-cutting scissors
- School ruler, preferably 18in (46cm) long
- Sharp pencil, a coloured pencil and eraser
- Fabric for the design ¼yd (0.25m) each of three different fabrics
- Fabric for border, backing and binding ¾yd (0.75m) in total
- Wadding (batting) 21in x 21in (53.3cm x 53.3cm)
- Quilting threads as desired

Size of block design (as in Fig 1b): 16in x 16in (40.6cm x 40.6cm).
Size of finished quilt: 20in x 20in (50.8cm x 50.8cm).

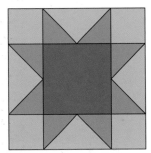

Fig 1a Ohio Star block

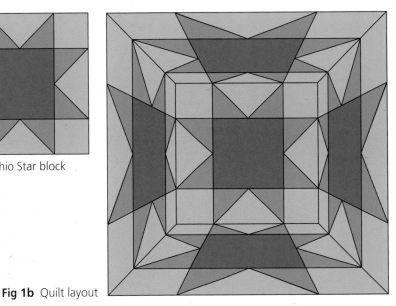

Fig 1b Quilt layout

Drafting Equipment

You will need some basic drafting equipment – nothing too troublesome. However, just for fun, if you want to experience being sneered at in a shop in the UK try asking for graph paper drawn up in inches rather than centimetres. Fortunately many quilt shops import graph pads from the USA for this purpose and may even sell large pieces by the sheet. Creative Grids UK (see details on page 117) sell pads of good cartridge paper measuring 16in x 16in (40.6cm x 40.6cm) drawn in a ¼in (6mm) grid, but if you get ambitious with future projects, you may have to stick several sheets together, which may not finish up as accurate as you would like. Consider

– shock, horror! – using metric graph paper for your design. If you work on a design based on 2in, 4in, 6in, 8in, 12in these will all translate approximately into easy metric equivalents as below.

2in	→	5cm
4in	→	10cm
6in	→	15cm
8in	→	20cm
12in	→	30cm

Just use the graph paper as it is marked and don't try to convert back into inches. If you choose graph paper that is marked both in centimetres and millimetres your work will be very accurate as the marked units are so closely spaced.

For drawing work it is more accurate to use a flat, school-type ruler rather than

a rotary ruler because the rotary rulers are far thicker and it is not easy to get the drawn lines in exactly the right position using them. A longer length is really useful, especially if you progress to larger designs, so try to get a school ruler that is at least 18in (46cm) long. Other than that, a sharp pencil (I use one of those propelling pencils that are always sharp), a good eraser and a sharp coloured pencil in any shade that shows up well on paper are all you need for the drafting session.

The freezer paper that is used for the piecing is made in America, where it was originally used for storing food in freezers, but we quilters use it in many kinds of patchwork. Most quilt shops sell it, either as a roll or in cut lengths.

'The perspective design shown here in fabric as a small wall hanging is called
Blue Perspective Stars. The centre Ohio Star has four side sections, each with
the star in perspective, giving a three-dimensional look to the design.'

Metric Tip

The conversion of 8in to metric is not exactly 20cm but if you are using metric graph paper I will give the approximate metric equivalents for you to follow – don't compare or try to convert, just follow all my metric alternative measurements which are printed in brackets after the Imperial measurements.

Drafting the Ohio Star block

1 The classic Ohio Star block is the first part to be drafted. The block measures 8in x 8in (20cm x 20cm). If your piece of graph paper measures 16in x 16in (40cm x 40cm) you will need to draw the Ohio Star to the left of the paper as shown in Fig 2 to allow room for the side perspective star. From the top left corner of the graph paper count down 4in (10cm). Mark this point with a dot.

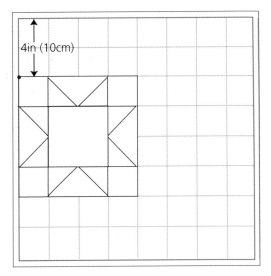

Fig 2

2 Draw a vertical line from the dot downwards 8in (20cm) long following Fig 3 below. Mark a dot at the end of this line. Now draw an 8in (20cm) box from this line as in Fig 4.

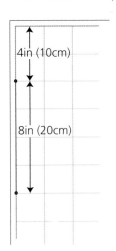

Fig 3

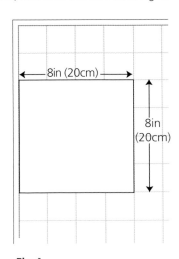

Fig 4

3 Mark along the top line of the box with a dot or small line 2in (5cm) from the left end and another dot 2in (5cm) from the right end as in Fig 5. Repeat this along the bottom line. Join the dots together vertically as in Fig 6.

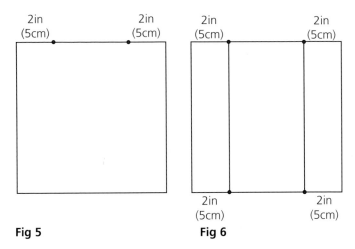

Fig 5   **Fig 6**

4 Turn the paper round through 90 degrees and repeat step 3 on the other two sides of the box (Fig 7). Each of these four new lines within the box should measure 8in (20cm). Measure each one and mark the exact midpoint, 4in (10cm) from the end, with a dot as in Fig 8.

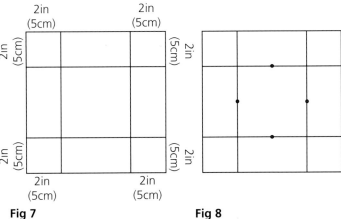

Fig 7   **Fig 8**

Tip

I have chosen the classic block Ohio Star for the centre of my perspective design because of its powerful graphic simplicity. It is based on a simple 4 x 4 unit grid, as are many other traditional patchwork blocks. The centre block used in the green design shown on page 62 has a slightly different arrangement of squares and triangles than Ohio Star, and there are many others that would fit the layout and could be tried in future projects.

5 Now join these dots to the outer box as shown in Fig 9. This completes the drafting of the Ohio Star block.

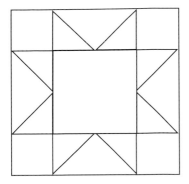

Fig 9 Ohio Star block

Drafting the perspective star

We all know that parallel lines, like the verges of a road, seem to get nearer to each other and finally converge as they run into the distance. We also can see that vertical objects like fence posts remain vertical at all times, even up the side of a hill or around a curve. The thing that changes is the distance between the posts, which appear to get closer together the further they are from the viewer. These aspects of perspective are used in the drafting of the distorted block. Look at Fig 10a below – the vertical sides of the distorted block (shown in red) are still upright. The horizontal sides now all converge in the centre of the original square block, the vanishing point. If the drawing is turned, as in Fig 10b, the perspective effect can be clearly seen. All we have to do now is draw it to get that effect in patchwork.

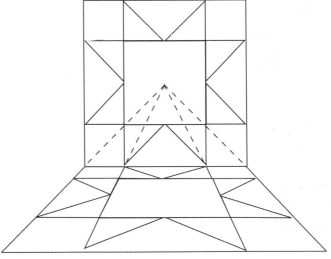

Fig 10b

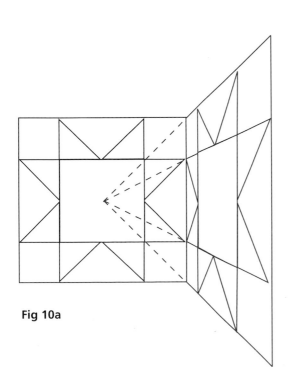

Fig 10a

1 The distance between the vanishing point in the centre of the original block and the side of the block is 4in (10cm). This measurement is used for the width of the distorted block. From the right side of the block measure 4in (10cm) and draw a vertical line parallel to it 16in (40cm) long as in Fig 11a. This is twice the length of the side of the original block. The midpoint of this line should be level with the midpoint of the side of the block.

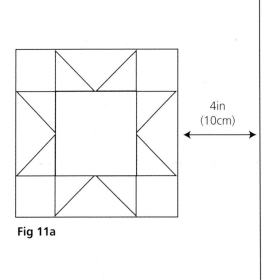

4in
(10cm)

Fig 11a

2 Mark this vertical line in quarters, each measuring 4in (10cm) as shown in Fig 11b.

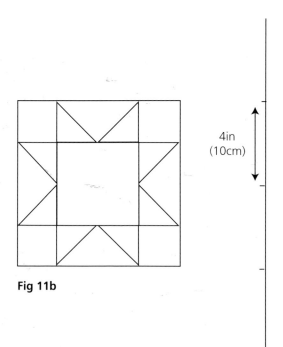

4in
(10cm)

Fig 11b

3 Now draw lines from the two corners of the block to the ends of the drawn line (Fig 12). This shape, called a trapezium, forms one side unit of the three-dimensional design.

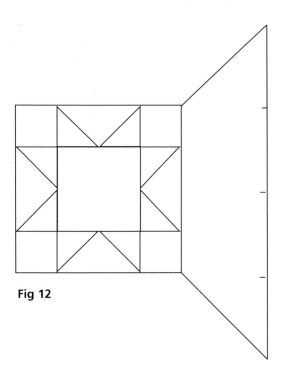

Fig 12

4 Draw lines from the corner of each of the two star points in the original block to the top and bottom marks on the longer outer line (Fig 13). If continued, these two lines would meet at the vanishing point in the centre of the original block, but we just need them to run across the new distorted block.

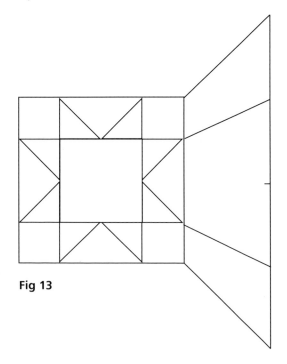

Fig 13

5 The other two main lines, which are vertical in the original block, are still vertical in the distorted version but the distances between them are not regular – they must get closer together towards the centre of the design to maintain true perspective. There is a simple way to do this that involves no hard sums at all. Turn the drawing round so that the trapezium is running along the bottom (Fig 14a). Place your ruler across the distorted block diagonally from top left corner to bottom right corner. Where the ruler crosses each of the two drawn lines within the block make a mark. We need to find the centre of the block too, so also draw a short line in the approximate centre of the block (Fig 14a). Repeat this diagonally in the other direction across the block (Fig 14b). The point where the two short lines cross marks the centre of the new block.

6 Place your ruler on the block horizontally to join the two top marked points and draw along it from side to side on the block (Fig 15a). Repeat this with the lower two marked points (Fig 15b). We now have the distorted block divided as the original was in Fig 7. Now all we need are the star points.

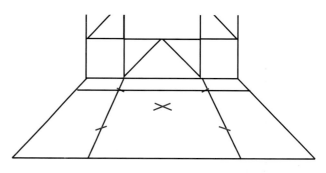

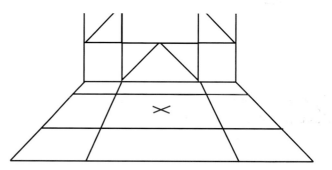

Fig 15a

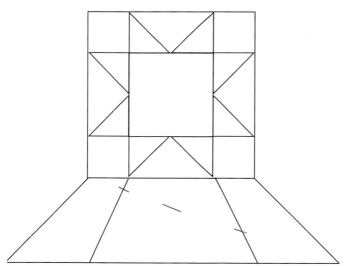

Fig 14a

Fig 15b

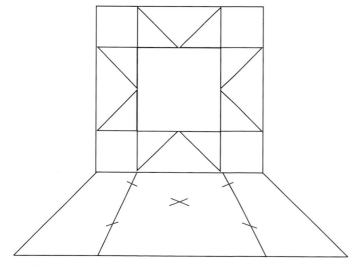

Fig 14b

7 To draw the star points we must find the midpoint of each of the internal long lines. Place the ruler across the whole design, from the centre vanishing point on the original block to the marked midpoint on the 16in (40cm) outer line. Where the ruler crosses each of the two internal lines on the distorted block make a mark (Fig 16a). These are the midpoints of each line. The other two mid points are not so easy to measure. The simplest way is to place the ruler across the distorted block horizontally through the marked centre point (where the two short drawn lines cross). Use the grid lines on the graph paper as a guide to place the ruler horizontally and parallel to the top and bottom lines of the distorted block – there probably won't be a graph line for you to follow, but keeping parallel with them will be a help. Where the ruler crosses each internal line in the block make a mark (Fig 16b).

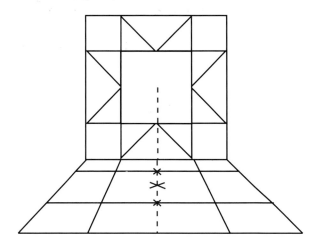

Fig 16a

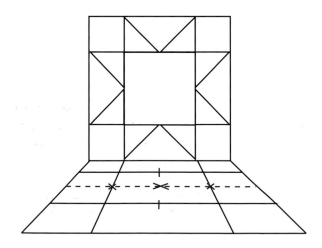

Fig 16b

8 Join these marks to the outer edges of the distorted block as shown in Fig 17 to complete the Ohio Star in perspective.

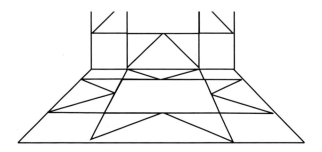

Fig 17

Tip

This is your master design to be used for reference and traced from using freezer paper. At this stage it is helpful to strengthen the drawn lines of the blocks and remove any construction lines to keep the design clearer.

Labelling the pieces

Number each piece as shown in Fig 18. Underline numbers <u>6</u> and <u>9</u> to avoid using them upside down by mistake. That's all the technical calculations and drafting done. Now it's on to the practical making of the design in fabric.

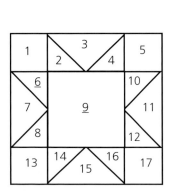

Fig 18

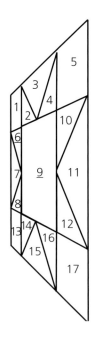

Making freezer paper templates

1 Start with just the distorted side section and trace the block onto freezer paper using a sharp pencil. Trace with the non-shiny side of the freezer paper *upwards*. The shiny side has been treated with wax and is difficult to draw on. The distorted side section must eventually be traced four times for the final design but I suggest making one section at a time in case you want to modify the design as it develops. Leave the original Ohio Star block until last – you may decide to use different fabric in this block or even not to piece it all but to have one square of fabric that is quilted in the star design. Number each piece *exactly* as shown in Fig 18.

2 Mark the grainline on each shape with a contrasting coloured pencil (see Tip below).

Tip

Keep the master design under the freezer paper. Turn the design so that all the parallel lines are horizontal (Fig 19). Place your ruler on the design horizontally and follow the lines of the graph paper to mark a horizontal grainline on each piece of the design. Kay Bruce's excellent tip is to add an arrowhead *at one end only* of each line, all pointing in the same direction as in Fig 19. This tip is invaluable as it helps you to position the strange shapes to make the design once they are cut up.

Fig 19

3 Cut out each freezer paper shape, cutting carefully along the drawn lines.

4 Take the fabric chosen for the background. Take the freezer paper pieces numbered 1, 3, 5, 7, 11, 13, 15 and 17. Press these shiny side *down* onto the *back* of the fabric, leaving at least ½in (1.3cm) between each shape. Place them so that the grainline arrow drawn on the paper matches the grain or weave of the fabric.

Tip

Freezer paper tends to lift off the fabric as you handle it, especially at the long sharp points. I use a really hot iron and press very firmly. I keep the iron by the machine while piecing and re-press any paper into position if it starts to lift off. Use assertive pressing – show no mercy…

5 Now cut out each piece with an exact ¼in (6mm) seam allowance on all sides, using a rotary cutter and ruler for accuracy. Trim any very long points to about ¼in (6mm) beyond the point of the paper piece (see Fig 20). The edge of the paper marks the stitching line. WS = wrong side of the fabric and RS = right side.

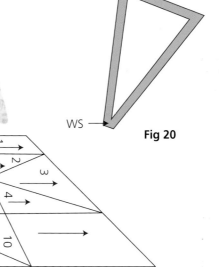

WS →   **Fig 20**

6 Now take the fabric to be used for the star points. Iron the freezer paper pieces 2, 4, 6, 8, 10, 12, 14 and 16 onto the *wrong* side of the fabric as before. Cut these out with a ¼in (6mm) seam allowance on all sides.

7 Finally iron piece 9 (the centre of the perspective star block design) onto the back of the chosen fabric and cut it out with a ¼in (6mm) seam allowance on all sides.

8 Arrange the design with the paper side facing *upwards* as in the original layout on the master design and check that it is correct. This is where those one-headed arrows are so useful – check that they are pointing in the same direction on each piece as you lay them out.

Tip

If you are a hand-worker, your freezer paper will probably come off the fabric as you handle it. Draw around the paper on each cut piece as closely to the edge as you can to transfer the stitching lines to the fabric. Remove the papers and then stitch together by hand, stitching just inside the drawn lines to keep the size of the design accurate. Machinists (this is my preferred way of freezer paper piecing) need an open foot on the machine to give a clear view ahead. I use the ¼in foot on my machine so I can follow the edge of the paper exactly.

Assembling the design

1 Pin pieces 1 and 2 together with right sides facing. Match the corners of the freezer paper with a pin at either end of the seam and line up the edges of the fabric. An extra pin or two along the seam may be needed on larger pieces. Stitch along the edges of the freezer paper including the seam allowance at either end. Finger-press the seam back towards piece 1.

Tip

If any freezer paper has been caught in the underneath seam, ease it out carefully. If it is caught really badly, unpick that small section and re-stitch it.

2 Place the joined section back in the design, paper side *upwards* to check that it is correct. Now pin and stitch piece 2 to piece 3 in the same way. Finger-press the seam back towards piece 2.

3 Pin and stitch piece 3 to 4 and then piece 4 to 5. This makes the top strip of the design. Now press firmly from both front and back to keep the freezer paper in place. Replace this section paper side *upwards* in the design and move on to the centre strip of the design.

4 Pin and stitch together piece 6 and 7. Finger-press the seam back towards piece 6 before adding piece 8. Finger-press this seam towards piece 8 to keep the layers flat. Place back in the design paper side *upwards*.

5 Leave piece 9 for the moment. Pin and stitch together pieces 10, 11 and 12 in the same way as 6, 7 and 8. Press in the same way. Join these two units to either side of piece 9 in the correct arrangement to complete the centre strip of this part of the design (Fig 21). Press firmly on both sides and replace paper side *upwards* in the design.

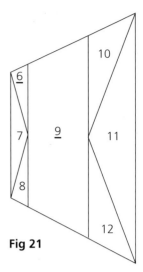

Fig 21

6 Pin and stitch together pieces 13, 14, 15, 16 and 17 in the same way as the top strip of pieces 1–5. Press firmly as before.

7 Finally, pin and stitch the three strips together to make one distorted side section of the design. Take care to match points and corners carefully.

Design choices

Before you rush on to make three more of these distorted blocks for the design, consider the other design options shown in Figs 22a, 22b and 22c. Having just one or two pieced side blocks and the others left as whole pieces with the design quilted on them is an option (Figs 22a and 22b). So is making two sections in one set of fabrics and two in a second set and arranging them as in Fig 22c, with side triangles of the background fabric to complete the design. Make your decisions and then construct the number of distorted blocks that you need plus the centre original Ohio Star if you want that in your design.

Tip

Assuming you are going to include the centre original Ohio Star block, do not be tempted to make this 8in x 8in (20cm x 20cm) block in the conventional way with rotary cutting and quick piecing as it may well not fit with the side sections.

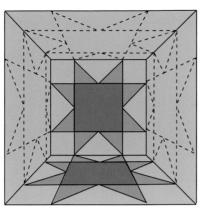

Fig 22a

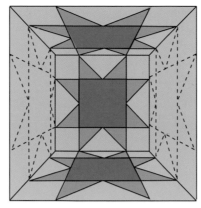

Fig 22b

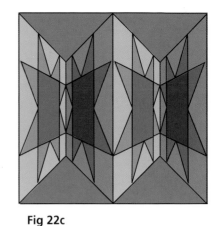

Fig 22c

8 Trace the centre Ohio Star block from the master drawing with freezer paper and piece the block following step 1 on page 71 onwards to step 7 opposite.

Tip

At this stage you are probably wrestling with rogue pieces of freezer paper which keep trying to detach themselves from the fabric. The temptation is to remove them all right now but try to keep them in place (use the hot iron again), as the paper does stop the edges of the fabric from stretching as you join the design together, especially on the diagonal mitred seams at each corner.

9 The next step in assembling the design is joining the sections. Arrange the five sections of the design in position as in Fig 1b on page 64. Join the two side sections to the centre block, matching corners and points carefully and stitching from corner to corner of the design, *not* into the seam allowance. In the same way stitch the top and bottom sections to the centre block, matching corners and seams carefully.

10 Finally, stitch the diagonal seams to complete the design, matching corners and seams carefully and stitching from the inner corner of the design towards the outer edge. If this is your complete design then remove the freezer paper and press the inner seams outwards from the centre. Press the diagonal seams open.

If you want to extend the design and make it larger, as Kate Badrick did on page 61, then leave the freezer paper in place for the moment and see Designing for Yourself, overleaf.

Adding a border

Do not be tempted to add a border with mitred corners, as this will continue the perspective effect. Instead, frame the design with a simple border with cornerstones as in Fig 23. This holds the perspective design in place and adds to the visual impact.

1 Cut four strips of the chosen border fabric, each 16½in x 2½in (41.2cm x 6.2cm). Cut four squares for the cornerstones, each 2½in x 2½in (6.2cm x 6.2cm). These can be the same fabric as the strips or a different fabric.

2 Pin and stitch a strip to either side of the design, stitching a ¼in (6mm) seam. Press the strips away from the block.

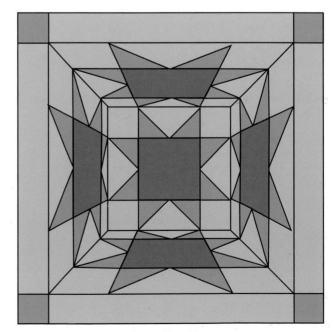

Fig 23

3 Pin and stitch a cut square of fabric to either end of the remaining two strips as in Fig 24. Press the seams towards the border strips. Now pin and stitch these strips to the top and bottom of the block, matching seams carefully. There, the patchwork is complete.

Fig 24

Finishing the quilt

All that remains is for you to layer the quilt with the wadding and backing fabric (see materials list on page 64 and the technique on page 112) and to quilt the design before finally binding the edges (see technique on page 114).

The design may be quilted by hand or machine as desired but I would recommend that you keep the quilting fairly low-key, limiting it to quilting in the ditch (in the seamlines) or echoing the geometric shapes of the distorted stars so that the quilting does not detract from the visual impact of the perspective design shapes.

Designing for yourself
Making a larger design

If desired, you could continue the perspective design outwards to create a larger design, as Kate Badrick did for her striking quilt shown on page 61. To draft the outer section of the design (shown in red in Fig 25), start with one side of the completed perspective block, a vertical line 16in (40cm) long. The distance between the central vanishing point and this side line is 8in (20cm). This measurement is used for the width of the outer, larger distorted block. From the right side of the vertical line measure 8in (20cm) and draw a vertical line parallel to it 32in (80cm) long. Follow the instructions in Drafting the Perspective Star step 8 beginning on page 68 to draft a larger version of the distorted block, changing the measurement in step 2 from 4in (10cm) to 8in (20cm). Make each side trapezium as before and stitch in place around the original perspective block.

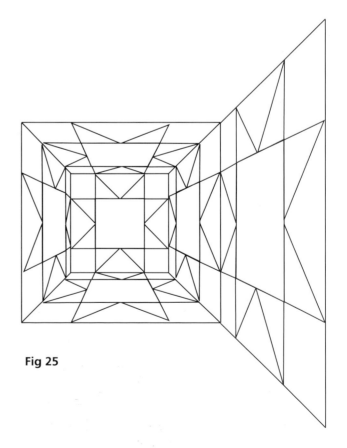

Fig 25

Using a different block

You could consider starting with a different block – nothing too complex, as simple, classic blocks make the biggest impact (see the example below). Draft it in exactly the same way as described for the Ohio Star. Just draw it out and see the effect, and then you can decide whether to take it further in fabric.

Drafting a tiled floor

1 A tiled floor in perspective can be drafted using the same principles – see picture below. With reference to Fig 26a construct the outer trapezium in the way described earlier (starting at step 1 page 68).

2 Divide line A into as many equal sections as you wish. Divide line B into the same number of sections as A (Fig 26b). Each section of line B will be twice the length of a section in line A. Join the marks together with lines as in Fig 26c.

3 Place a ruler diagonally across the trapezium from corner to corner. Mark where the ruler crosses each drawn inner line. Repeat this on the other diagonal (Fig 26d).

4 Join the marks horizontally to complete the perspective grid (Fig 26e).

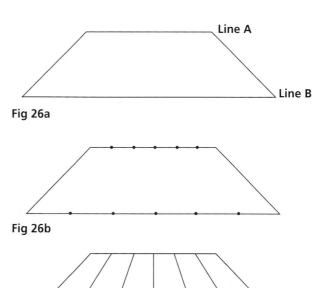

Line A

Line B

Fig 26a

Fig 26b

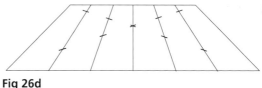

Fig 26c

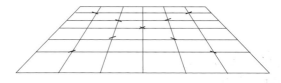

Fig 26d

Fig 26e

"I hope these instructions have been easy to follow and you have enjoyed creating perspective effects in fabric. If you feel inspired to go on to make original and stunning quilts that sweep the board at major quilt shows, remember, you owe it all to me…"

Fresh Vintage™
by Joanna Figueroa, USA

For me, quilting is a perfect combination of art and practicality. As I work, I can be totally creative, engrossed in the aspects of design, of colour palette, of proportion. At the same time I am aware that I am being totally utilitarian, knowing that the article I create can be used not only as a piece of art but also as something to keep someone warm!

Vintage quilts and unusual vintage colour combinations inspire most of my designs. I can't seem to go anywhere without seeing patterns or colour combinations for potential quilts – in nature, in greetings cards and wrapping paper, even in dishware and pottery. Our Fig Tree designs have a soft, vintage feel about them, updated with clean, fresh colours and I call our look Fresh Vintage™. We use a cream base for all of our collections and then work to create a palette of warm, vibrant tones that use today's fabric trends while still staying true to our traditional colour roots.

My favourite quilts utilize a patchwork design that shows off the fabric and colour. I am not drawn to complex designs unless they truly showcase a fabric combination in a way that another pattern would not. Whether vintage or contemporary, soft or bold, masculine or romantic, I believe that any feeling can be communicated through a well-chosen palette of colour, pattern, and texture.

Besides quilting, I enjoy searching for vintage textiles, antique toys, painted furniture, and ceramics – anything that seems loved and well used. My husband Eric says I have an unnatural love of bowls and painted chairs! My love of antique quilts was the inspiration for the quilt shown opposite.

"I believe that any feeling can be communicated through a well-chosen palette of colour, pattern, and texture."

Over the centuries hexagons have been a very popular way to make a variety of designs in traditional quilts and the looks have varied from very classic to quite contemporary. This design uses the warm tones so characteristic of our Fig Tree designs.

Joanna Figueroa Inspirations

When I bought my first small, antique quilt at a garage sale (a bubblegum pink wishbone pattern baby quilt), I fell in love with the art of quilting. But when I made my first simple quilt, I fell in love with the process of quilting itself. After that I knew that there was something about the creation and history of quilting that spoke to the deepest part of me. It was as if something inside of me had clicked.

Inspiration is Everywhere

A question I am often asked is how I can continue to come up with new designs for patterns and fabric. I always answer that it is not something I set out to do on purpose; my imagination generates new design ideas from everything I see around me. Most of the fabric lines, as well as Fig Tree & Co. patterns, are inspired by and based on various vintage items that I have found and fallen in love with. Some of the best inspirations have come from the most unlikely places – the inside of a vintage hat box, a very small remnant of an antique piece of fabric, a tattered children's book illustration… You never know where the next inspiration might come from, so I'm always on the lookout for interesting colour combinations on old items and junk finds. For me the best treasure hunts are at flea markets and estate sales, where you never know what you are going to find. For example, at one flea market I found some wonderful old tin trays. The colours on them create such a wonderful nostalgic feel and I know those trays or the colours on them are going to be the inspiration for some fabrics or quilt patterns one day. I feel I have more design ideas in my head than I will ever be able to put on paper. Sometimes that is wonderful and sometimes it keeps me up at night (and drives my husband a little bit batty!).

Creating Feelings with Fabric

What I am always trying to do is to communicate a 'feeling' with fabric, something that will inspire other people to create something cherished, something that will bring them joy. The name we give to our fabrics usually incorporates either the inspiration item or a feeling that I hope the colour palette communicates.

I'm often asked how I get that signature creamy, soft 'Fig Tree' look. At trade shows, the comment I get most often is, 'It feels so warm in here – can I just lie down in your booth and rest?' I am always glad to hear that because it is exactly the feeling I hope to convey with our fabrics and patterns.

Fabric and Colour Selection

When I started designing patterns, the comments I heard most often were, 'What line of fabric did you make that from?' and 'Where did you find that great colour combination?' Whenever I worked on patterns for Fig Tree & Co, I kept coming up with colour combinations in my imagination that I just couldn't find in real fabric. I longed to create my own fabric to express those combinations. The first quilt market that Fig Tree & Co attended was a resounding success and during the following year, I began working with Moda. Designing fabric was a natural outgrowth of our mutual love of those vintage colour combinations we were working so hard to achieve. Given my background in political science and theology, no one would have ever guessed that this is where I would have ended up but I can't think of anything I'd rather be doing – I feel as if I've come home.

The most important thing to learn in the world of colour is to know what you like. This might sound like a simple idea but the truth is that most people, including quilters, aren't sure of what style they like, what colour combinations they like and so they struggle to find palettes that please them. To figure out what you like, you need to start looking everywhere to see what kinds of colour or colour palettes appeal to you in various arenas of your life. Look not only at fabrics but at home decorating colours, your dishware colours, colours on stationery or clothes. Soon enough you will begin to see your own 'trends'. Don't be afraid of whatever colour palettes you are drawn to, whether they are bright or muted. This will be your first step in choosing well for your quilt projects.

This quilt pattern, called Snowflake Rose, was inspired by my desire to create fabric snowflakes that would not be appliquéd but pieced using only simple and traditional strip piecing techniques. Using several different red prints from our Gypsy Rose fabric collection and my favourite cream from that group, the snowflakes turned out just like I had hoped. To me they feel like each one is different and unique even though they are technically all identical. One day I would love to make an aqua blue version of this quilt – winter personified.

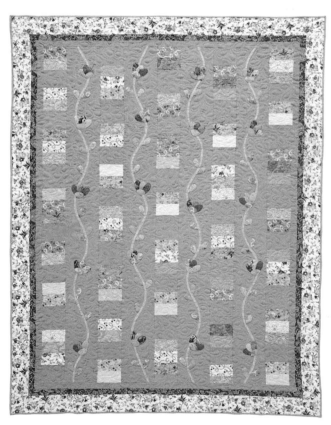

Inspired by the Japanese trend of using soft greys to add vintage flavour to brighter colours, this is definitely one of my current favourite quilts. Sophisticated due to that grey linen background, Twilight Bloom uses a variety of prints from my Gypsy Rose collection and achieves a soft, mellow look that is both a bit trendy and totally unique. Definitely a departure from our standard cream-based quilt, it has an across-the-board appeal.

Choosing a Palette

I know that this might not be a popular sentiment, but I really believe that a finished quilt will only be as good as the initial colour palette choices. That still leaves a huge amount of room for interpretation, for colour preferences, for inspiration. But regardless of what kind of colour palette you like to work with, I think that the process of choosing your palette is extremely important. One of my favourite quotes is from Georgia O'Keeffe. 'I found I could say things with colour and shapes that I couldn't say any other way – things I had no words for.'

For me a particular colour combination or inspiration is where I always start. The colour combinations of old drawings and vintage illustrations have always fascinated me. For whatever reason, we don't often put together such wonderful and unusual combos in this day and age. If you look at old children's book drawings, you'll notice that they often use colours that were just a little bit 'off' as we would say today – not the colour combination that you might expect to see. I love to try to capture that vintage feel, which often seems so elusive today.

To do that, I always start with a cream base. What I mean by this is that many fabrics have a white base, making them cooler in appearance. Their basic undertone is white or grey. Some fabrics even have a specifically cool base, a blue tone to whatever colour palette is on that fabric. I stay away from those fabrics. Fabrics with a cream base, on the other hand, with cream as their lightest tone, are warmer in general tone and hue. Reds are more tomato reds, orangey and soft. Greens are more limey or chartreuse. Blues are more aqua, with slightly green overtones. Pinks are more likely to be peach and apricot. Even blacks and greys can be warm or cold. You'd be amazed if you started laying black fabrics next to each other, to see the amount of difference there is between a warmer and a cooler black. Many fabrics often have other colours in them besides the main colourway. These accent colours will also add or subtract from the overall warm feeling of the fabric. Train your eye to look at all the colour in a particular fabric. Try looking at each colour in the colour wheel as having the potential to be warm or cool.

Working with the new Moda precut fabrics is a design challenge that I always enjoy. I am constantly trying to create quilts that look like they came from our personal stash as opposed to being based on all one line. Figgy Pudding, above, is one of those projects that I began working on using a Moda Layer Cake™ and Charm Pack and loved how it evolved. I added in some of my favourites from previous lines and the result is soft, scrappy and looks like it came straight from my grandma's attic. Folks love the versatility of this quilt!

Inspired by branches of spring blooms outside my kitchen window, this Les Fleurs pattern is definitely an heirloom classic. One of two quilts in this pattern, the petals float across the fabric as the delicate birds perch in various positions throughout the project. A soft, simply pieced background give this appliqué project added depth and movement and the appliqué feels both traditional and completely fresh at the same time.

Another principle that I often work with is that yellow goes with everything! Many years ago, I heard another designer say this in a workshop on brights and contemporary fabrics. The same principle has translated very well into vintage colour combinations. There is no colour on the colour wheel that looks bad with yellow. Now, of course the yellow I mean is a soft, butter yellow or a warm, mustard yellow or a strong cream yellow. These yellows often form the basis of the colour palettes I work with. The strength of the yellow depends on what type of a feeling I am trying to convey or what type of colour combination I am trying to create.

Lastly, I always try to add some colours to 'ground' my quilt. Most quilters stay within the medium range of tones, never branching out into true lights or true darks. I've never struggled with adding cream and ivory as my lights but learning how to add good dark browns, warm blacks and soft greys has brought a strong grounding element to my designs. These colours give your eye somewhere to rest as they move around the myriad of other colours in your project. Try using some of these principles in your next quilt project and see where your imagination can take you.

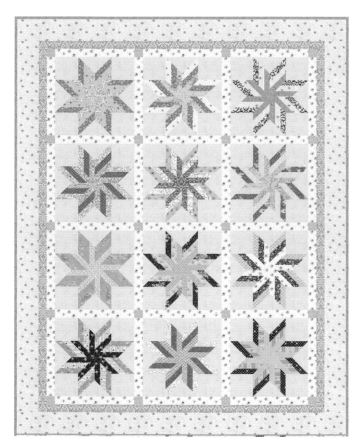

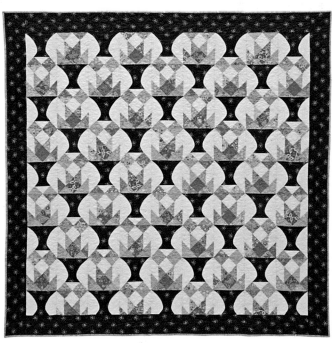

Created using our Patisserie collection from Moda, Sweet Sugar Swirls is my take on those traditional twirling star blocks from the 1800s with a fresh Fig update. The quilt is created with one Honeybun™, one of the newest Moda precuts, and three to four background and setting fabrics. I created a way of making them with no special techniques or y-seams, so that way I actually enjoyed making the blocks! What could be more simple? Soft and vibrant all at the same time, these stars appear to be moving as you follow them around the project.

One of my favourite things to do is re-fashioning and recalculating traditional blocks made with traditional techniques to make them accessible to everyday quilters. This block was fashioned after a popular Candy Dish block, popular in the early part of the last century. Usually made with an entire array of templates, we worked and reworked the blocks of Fresh Vintage Issue: Fig Parfait to make them with only one basket appliqué template and all standard piecing besides that. This one was definitely a mathematical challenge but well worth the results I think. The strong plum with the soft remaining colours creates such a wonderful secondary pattern throughout the quilt.

Twinkling Stars

One of the many types of quilts that seem to surface in almost every book dedicated to antique quilts are hexagon quilts from the 1800–1900s. While studying antique quilts, particularly these hexagon quilts, I became fascinated with the designs that could be created depending on the tone of the 'in-between' triangles. As I played with various colours and placements, I decided to focus this pattern on the wonderful stars that were created by the background triangles instead of the hexagon blocks themselves. I love the somewhat unexpected result. Whereas traditional hexagon quilts were always made with templates and used time consuming Y seams, this pattern uses a simple, unique way that does not require either method. Simple cutting and strip piecing takes care of those traditional methods and helps to create a quilt that is both easy to construct and intricate to look at. The project was designed using imperial measurements and although metric equivalents have been provided, the best results will be obtained using imperial.

Size of finished block: 7¼in x 8½in (18.4cm x 21.6cm).
Size of finished quilt: 71¼in x 74in (181cm x 188cm).

Materials

- Twelve fabrics in assorted colours each 4½in (11.43cm), or ⅛yd (0.12m) of each
- Brown fabric for triangles and inner brown border 1¼yd (1.2m) in total
- Cream background fabric and inner cream border 2¾yd (2.6m) in total
- Light floral or mosaic pattern fabric for outer border 1⅜yd (1.5m) in total
- Wadding (batting) 75in x 78in (109cm x 198cm) approx
- Backing fabric 75in x 78in (109cm x 198cm) approx
- Brown floral fabric for binding eight 2¼in (5.7cm) wide strips, ⅝yd (0.6m) in total
- Quilter's ruler with 60 degree marking
- Quilting threads as desired

Tip

Even though precise measurements are given for all the borders in this project it is highly recommend that you measure your own quilt and cut your own size borders. With all these triangles and bias, your measurements might be different from mine.

Cutting the fabrics

1 Begin by cutting twelve 4½in (11.4cm) wide strips from an assortment of fabrics. You will need a total of 117 colour triangles. Cut twelve triangles from each strip – this will give you more than you need but you will have a wider choice of colours.

2 Cut sixteen 4½in (11.4cm) wide strips from the cream background fabric. You will need a total of 211 cream triangles for the quilt.

3 Cut six 4½in (11.4cm) wide strips from the brown fabric. You will need a total of 104 brown triangles.

4 Cut six 2in (5cm) wide cream strips for the inner border. Piece these together in a single length and then cut into two

58½in (148.6cm) lengths for the side borders and two 58¾in (149cm) lengths for the top and bottom borders (see Tip above).

5 Cut six 2in (5cm) wide brown strips for inner brown border. Piece these together in a single length and then cut into two 61½in (156.2cm) lengths for side borders and two 61¾in (156.8cm) lengths for the top and bottom borders.

6 Cut eight 5½in (14cm) wide light floral or mosaic pattern strips for the outer border. Piece these together in a single length and then cut into two 64½in (163.8cm) lengths for the side borders and two 71¾in (182.2cm) lengths for the top and bottom borders.

7 Cut eight 2¼in (5.7cm) wide brown floral strips for binding the quilt.

"I love that in this quilt, the main attraction is the secondary pattern created by the brown triangles! The stars just dance and sparkle when I look at them."

8 Now, using a quilter's ruler with a 60 degree marking, cut all of your 4½in (11.4cm) strips into 60 degree triangles, as shown in Fig 1 a–c below (see also the Tip below). Each block will be made using one colour and cream triangles. The brown triangles will become the 'in-between' triangles that surround the blocks. The blocks are then assembled in rows (described in step 2).

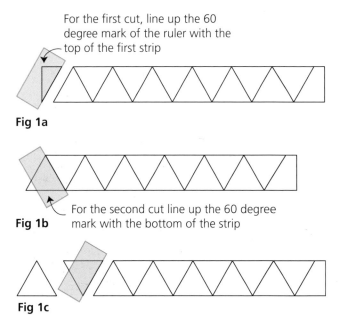

For the first cut, line up the 60 degree mark of the ruler with the top of the first strip

Fig 1a

For the second cut line up the 60 degree mark with the bottom of the strip

Fig 1b

Fig 1c

Fig 1a–c Cutting 60 degree triangles

Tip

These triangles are equilateral but only one side is a straight edge and the other two are bias. As you cut them and place them on a pile, make sure that you lay them all in the same direction and you mark your pile in some way so you know which edge is the straight edge. You will need to place this straight edge at the top/bottom of your block and keep your bias edges on the sides when piecing. If you don't do this, you will have difficulty with the fabric pieces stretching.

Piecing the triangles

1 Assemble the triangles into hexagon halves. Start by laying the triangles out in the placement that they need to be. First lay triangle 2 on top of triangle 1, right sides together, matching them up *exactly*. Sew together along the right side as shown in Fig 2a. Finger-press to the right (see Tip above step 2). Add triangle 3 to the right side aligned at the top and projecting at the base by ¼in (6mm) – see Fig 2b, so that when it is sewn and opened up its edges will match triangle 1. Add a brown triangle in the same way (Fig 2c).

align triangle 1 and triangle 2 right sides together

dog ear

Triangle 2

Triangle 1

WS

Fig 2a

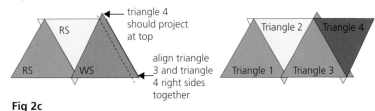

align triangle 2 and triangle 3 right sides together

triangle 3 should project at base

WS

RS

Triangle 2

Triangle 1 Triangle 3

Fig 2b

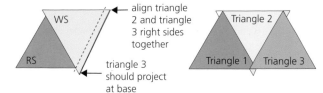

triangle 4 should project at top

align triangle 3 and triangle 4 right sides together

RS

RS WS

Triangle 2 Triangle 4

Triangle 1 Triangle 3

Fig 2c

Fig 2a–c Piecing the triangles together

Tip

With this quilt it is simple to finger-press each section as you work on it. After you sew triangle 2 to triangle 1, finger-press it to the right. Add triangle 3, offset as shown in Fig 2b, and finger-press it to the right. Add a brown triangle, offset as in Fig 2c and finger-press it to the right. Continue like this across the row and then iron once you have sewn the whole row.

2 To avoid working with tricky Y seams the hexagons are assembled in rows. Begin to assemble them as shown in Figs 3a and 3b below, assembling two rows at a time – the top and bottom row of one full row of hexagons. Do not assemble the actual hexagons together. Be sure to alternate how the blocks are laid out, so that every other block has the colour in the 'up' position and alternate blocks have colour in the 'down' position.

colour up (i.e., coloured triangle uppermost)

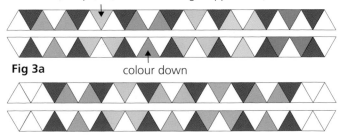

Fig 3a colour down

Fig 3b Joining the rows

3 Assemble the hexagon cream and brown triangles to create four rows of six blocks and three rows of five blocks. Finish the five-block rows with cream triangles on each end (see Fig 4). Now join the rows together, alternating the two types of rows.

4 Using the leftover cream and brown triangles, create a 'top' and 'bottom' row. Use six brown triangles and twenty-one cream triangles to create each row (Fig 4). The assembly for these rows is exactly the same as the five-block rows except that there is no colour added. All the blocks are made from cream triangles. Add one of these rows to the top as shown in Fig 4 and then add one to the bottom (shown in Fig 5).

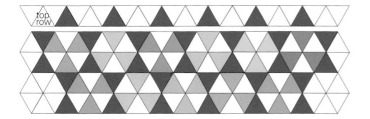

Fig 4 Adding the top row. Repeat the process with the bottom row

5 Trim the cream triangles that extend on the left and right sides to create a straight edge (Fig 5). It is important to remember to trim a ¼in (6mm) away from the points so as to still have a seam allowance when adding the borders.

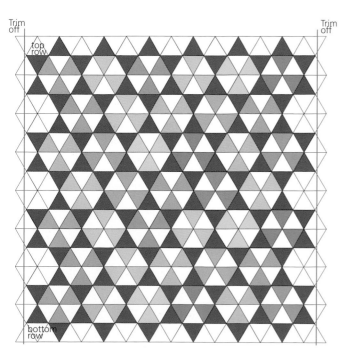

Fig 5 Trimming the edges

Adding the borders

1 Using ¼in (6mm) seams, add the inner cream borders to the left and right sides and press seams outwards. Add the inner cream borders to the top and bottom and press outwards (Fig 6).

2 In the same way add the inner brown borders. Now repeat the border process with the pink outer border.

Fig 6 Adding the borders

Finishing the quilt

1 Make a quilt sandwich of the top, wadding (batting) and backing (see page 112) and then quilt as you desire. When quilting is complete, remove any tacking (basting). Trim the excess wadding and backing fabric even with the edge of the quilt top.

2 Join the eight 2¼in (5.7cm) wide strips for the binding (see page 110) and bind the quilt as described on page 114. Label your quilt to finish (see page 114).

"This quilt is the ideal project to experiment with your own colour preferences. Don't be afraid of whatever colour palettes you are drawn to, whether they are bright or muted."

Folk Art Collage
by Janet Bolton, UK

The inspiration for my work comes from all walks of life – from my memory and imagination, from direct visual experience and from the very material I have chosen to work with. All of these play a part, and a combination of these sources can quite often come together in the same piece.

Looking back, I realize that the same working methods that absorbed me when playing as a child, for example, making imaginary gardens with flowerheads, sticks and stones, are still the methods I use in building up an idea for my collages today. By this I mean that an idea is developed with the actual fabrics that will be incorporated in the work, rather than working out composition, colourways and so on in another medium and then transposing those ideas into fabric.

Describing some of the ideas behind the examples shown here and overleaf will, I hope, give you direct visual insight into my ideas and my working methods and allow you to use the ideas as a springboard to create your own individual pieces of work. The Flowers at the Window project on pages 92–95 gives general guidance on creating my style of folk art collages, but always be guided by your own instincts and artistic sense.

"Fabric is my main source of inspiration. I enjoy it for its own sake, loving its texture, weave, colour, pattern, the juxtaposition of which is essential in my work."

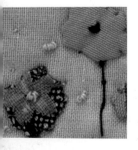
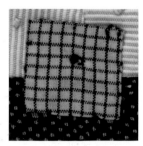

The project in this chapter, Flowers at the Window, shows how important the placing of each element in relation to its neighbour is to create a pleasing final result. Even the picture mount plays a part in the balance of the final piece.

Janet Bolton Inspirations

There is no doubt that fabric is my main source of inspiration – its texture, weave, colour and pattern, plus the juxtaposition of different fabrics – I think it's important to work with a selection of particular pieces of fabric from the very start of a project. The placement of the various elements in a design is important to create a balanced and pleasing piece. My work is more concerned with picture making in whatever medium than traditional patchwork, with needle-turn appliqué playing an important part in the creation of the pictures.

Green Bird in a Square Garden

This piece reflects what is the main source of inspiration for my work, the fabric itself. My more abstract pieces are often composed to allow the fabric to speak for itself without imagery. Yet here I couldn't resist adding the green bird at the last moment.

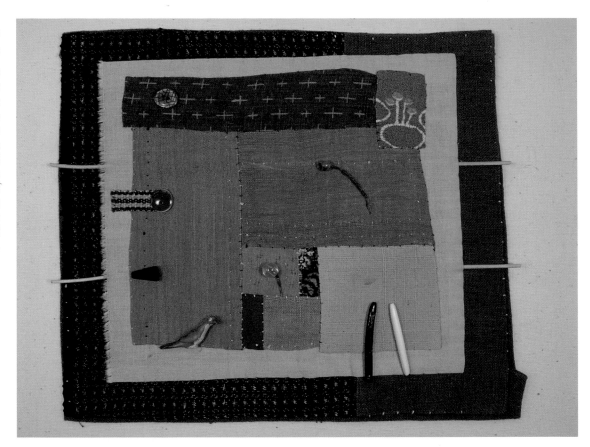

The Cowslip, the Castle and the Cabbage White

Here an actual landscape inspired the work – the view from the workroom at Cowslip workshops in Cornwall, UK, where I teach. This piece was built up from my memory. When working with direct visual experience I don't want to let accurate reality become as important as the composition of the picture, the 'atmosphere' I want to create or the way I remember it.

One Boat on a Calm Day

Here, again, in real life I have not observed this particular configuration, indeed some of the elements are purely abstract and are placed for the balance of the overall piece. There is a play between flat pattern and a sense of perspective.

Two Sheep Watching

Visits to the north of England, where I was born, usually inspire a new series of northern scenes. Again you can see a complete disregard for perspective – just how big should those sheep be? Yet having said this I did intend to create some suggestion of space, landscape and distance.

Wrapped up Warm

My grandchildren are a constant source of inspiration. Pictures such as this are never accurate portraits, just an idea. This I think is why other people see their own children in my pieces (although I do not plan it in this way). Often the comment is, 'But it is just her (or him)!'. Maybe this is also why others can read landscape into my unrealistic interpretations of them. It allows people to read their own stories into a piece of work.

Watching the Sandcastle Disappear

Sometimes a piece of fabric can bring memories flooding back. An ongoing beach series was originally inspired by a gift of scraps of old fabric, which reminded me of hand-me-down dresses worn on the beach. This introduction of memory, of a past use, is very satisfying and links work to age-old traditions, which to me is very enjoyable.

Wild Flowers by the Window

The background fabric used for this was an old handkerchief. I wanted this delightful fabric to remain important so I added a few delicate stitches to its pattern and kept the composition very simple. The delicate hankie had a light, summery feel and wild flowers seemed a suitable subject to complement this. I used an old Japanese fabric for the vase. Small, needle-turned flowers and a couple of added objects completed the piece.

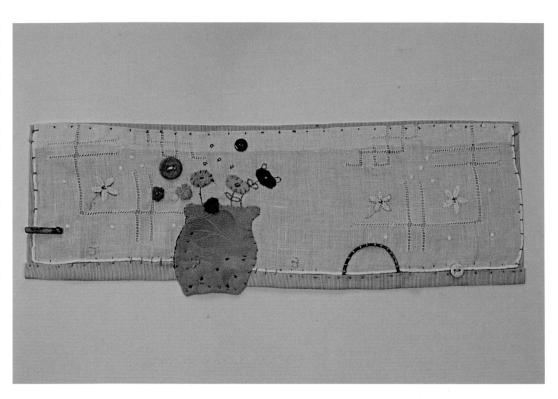

Simple Flowers

This picture is another example of the same theme of wild flowers by a window but this time using a different set of fabrics. For this one I used an old French fabric for the flower vase.

Flowers at the Window

Flowers have been depicted from time immemorial and in every medium, and as you will have seen they are a recurring theme in my work, linking in to my love of folk art. For this collage I enjoyed suggesting a landscape setting for the imagery – a recurring idea that I play around with all the time. These landscapes are rarely accurate interpretations of something I have observed, but are rather images I create in my own imaginary world. You will probably already have fabrics in your own collection that you could use for this picture and easily be able to source others. The needle-turn appliqué will be easier if you select fine, thin fabrics. See page 110 for advice on the technique of needle-turn appliqué.

Size of finished picture (including mount): 12½in x 13in (32cm x 33cm).

Materials
Fabric amounts are only approximate as your requirements will vary depending on the picture you create, but mostly only scraps are needed
- Two pieces of fabric for the background
- Fabric for the border strips
- Selection of fabric scraps for the hill, vase and flowers
- Backing fabric 15in x 16in (38cm x 40.5cm) approximately
- Small section of basket maker's cane (optional)
- Beads and buttons as desired
- Sewing threads

Creating the background and borders

1 Join your background pieces of fabric together, press the seam and also press in the outer edges, as shown in Fig 1.

2 Join the border strips to create a top border and a bottom border, allowing for the side extensions (Fig 2a and 2b).

background fabric pieces

RS

Fig 1

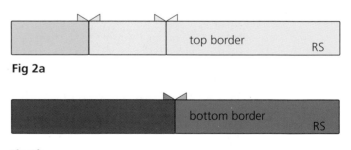

top border

RS

Fig 2a

bottom border

RS

Fig 2b

"In these more affluent times it is very pleasing to carry
on the make-do-and-mend mentality and in this way
continue old traditions."

3 Placing the fabrics right sides together, sew the top border to the background (Fig 3).

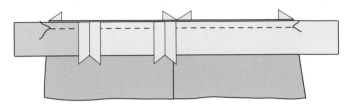

Fig 3

4 Press under the top edge of the border and turn the extended edges back on to themselves (Fig 4).

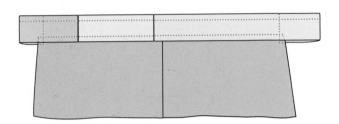

Fig 4

Tip

I find that old, well-worn fabrics are the easiest to work with as they turn under well and make the appliqué easier.

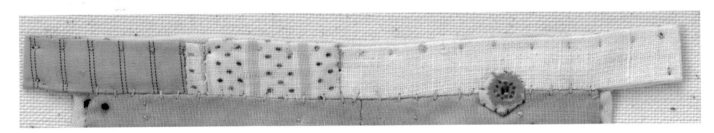

5 Place the 'hill' into position on the background, with the top and outer edge pressed into place (Fig 5).

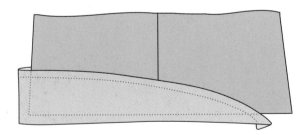

Fig 5

6 Now place the bottom border into position over the hill, just as you did for the top, and press open.

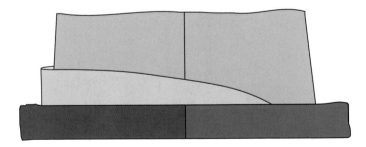

Fig 6

Adding the appliqué

1 Cut out and place your fabric shapes for the flowers, vase and other shapes, trying a variety of different fabrics to see how they look together and on your background – use your own judgement about what looks 'right'. Pin the shapes into position and sew into place using needle-turn appliqué (see page 110), altering the shapes as desired to please you.

Fig 7

2 Finally, referring to the picture on page 93 if you wish, or making your own decisions, add any top stitches to be seen, any buttons, beads and so on. I added a small section of basket maker's cane, cut to the size I required, but you could omit this or use something different.

Tip

The small elements added at this final stage can make all the difference and is why I find working this way so exciting. Top stitches can be added where, originally, the joining stitch occurred. These stitches will add to the composition and can draw the eye to a particular area.

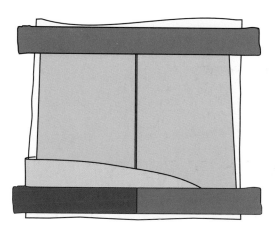

Tip

You can see from the small sections shown here that it would be difficult to 'compose' with seam allowances in place as the shapes overlap and you cannot evaluate the spaces between each flower. So, using your compositional shape as a template, cut a larger piece out of the same fabric, replace the first and turn under a little at a time. You may want to alter the shape a little as you work.

3 Place the collage on to your chosen backing fabric, with wrong sides together (Fig 8). Turn in the backing edges so that a little can be seen (see the detail pictures).

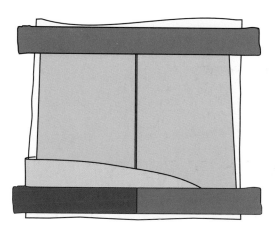

Fig 8

"It can be very liberating working the way I do and I hope you have enjoyed not being a slave to the ruler – at least for a little while."

Feathered Star Patchwork
by Marsha McCloskey, USA

I can barely remember a time when I was not interested in quilts and quiltmaking – the sheer creativity of the craft, its intricacies, the gorgeous fabrics and the fascinating effects that can be achieved. Originally, I was a graphic artist, having majored in graphic arts in college, but in 1969 I turned from printmaking to quiltmaking. I sold my earliest quilting efforts at the weekly Saturday market in Eugene, Oregon, but of course, as I sold quilts, potholders, baby blocks and the like, I then had to make more to replace them! In this way I developed and practised my skills as a seamstress and fabric artist. For many years in the Northwest and California I made patchwork gift items for gift shops and craft fairs. In 1975 I began teaching quiltmaking at a local quilt store.

Today I specialize in Feathered Star designs, because for me, Feathered Star quilts stand out as benchmarks of achievement in traditional pieced patchwork. The quilts created with these complex stars are generally made with the utmost care and the finest fabrics. Their twinkling beauty is achieved by edging geometric star patterns with small triangles called 'feathers'. Since 1981 I have written or co-authored over 25 books on quiltmaking but Feathered Star and other traditional pieced designs continue to hold a fascination for me. I hope that you will agree once you have made the Lady of the Lake project described in this chapter.

The quilt, shown opposite, has a Le Moyne Star centre. In this star the side triangle is equal to half of the corner square, so essentially the same block will fit in each position. Here, the small Lady of the Lake blocks (with lots of triangles) fit evenly around the large centre star. The result is a block with the twinkling look of a Feathered Star.

*"If you love precision piecing,
you will have a great time
making this striking quilt."*

This stunning quilt makes a wonderful wall hanging or could be the centre of a larger, medallion-style quilt. It is basically a scrap quilt and is a great project to make from your stash of fabrics. Templates are used to piece the quilt accurately.

Marsha McCloskey Inspirations

I first became fascinated by Feathered Stars in the 1980s when I went to the Houston Quilt Festival in Texas, where Karey Bresenhan (now President of Quilts Inc) had an exhibit of traditional red and green quilts. It was breathtaking to see all the designs worked in the same colours. My favourite quilt was a star pattern labelled 'Feathered Star'. I was smitten and sketched the block so I could research it and make the design myself.

Now, in 1983, it was possible to own all the quilt books and in my quilt library I found a picture of the design I sought: it was called not 'Feathered Star' but 'Radiant Star' – but there was no pattern for it. In my search I found that there were hundreds of different Feathered Star blocks and that Feathered Star is not just one block design but a whole category. I began collecting the designs and eventually wrote the book I wanted to read when I first became interested in the stars. *Feathered Star Quilts* was published in 1987 by That Patchwork Place and is now out

of print, but I continue to work on new Feathered Star designs and teach other quilters about them.

The Lady of the Lake Feathered Star Wall quilt shown on page 97 was inspired by a quilt shown by a quilt dealer at Houston Quilt Festival in the mid 1990s. I was taken by the unusual fact that the corner squares of the block had feather triangles on all four sides. Placing Lady of the Lake blocks around a large Le Moyne Star was an interesting way to achieve a Feathered Star look and the quilt featured in this chapter is the result. I made it to showcase my first line of Staples background fabrics in 1996.

The 15in (38cm) Radiant Star block in the quilt below is one of the easiest of Feathered Stars to make. The pattern for this and the Le Moyne Star opposite can be found in my book *Feathered Star Quilt Blocks I* (see page 117 for details). I made this quilt in 1993. The overall quilt size is 72½in (184cm) square and it was hand quilted by Freda Smith. From the collection of Barb Vose.

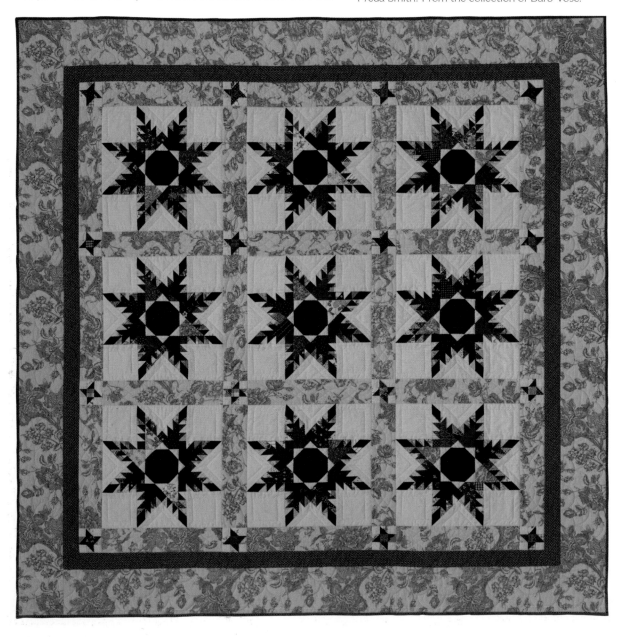

Feathered Star designs achieve their energy and sparkle with the use of highly contrasting fabrics – light lights and dark darks. This antique quilt is a Feathered Star variation but its size and provenance are unknown.

This Feathered Star block finishes at 23⅛in (58.7cm). The larger the star, the larger the centre square or octagon, and the more opportunity we have to add piecing. The Le Moyne Star is a traditional treatment but hundreds of centre variations are possible.

Lady of the Lake Quilt

This Feathered Star design is visually arresting and lends itself to a wide variety of colour and tone combinations. It has a Le Moyne Star as the central block. This is surrounded by side and corner units, each edged with strip-pieced feather units. Three borders, two of them pieced, finish the design. The full quilt is shown opposite and its diagrammatic layout is shown in Fig 1 below. The project was designed using imperial measurements and although metric equivalents have been provided, I urge you to use imperial for accurate results. Read all the instructions through before you start preparing fabric.

Size of finished quilt: 41in x 41in (104cm x 104cm)

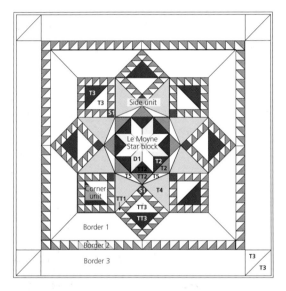

Fig 1 Quilt layout

Materials

Total fabric amounts are given here – refer to the two cutting charts (right) for details

- Medium and dark-coloured prints 1¼yd (1.25m) in total, in assorted colours including pinks, reds, purples, greens, blues, greys, a brown, a gold and a navy – you will need a 9in (23cm) square of each colour, plus enough extra for other shapes in the star
- Assorted light background prints 1¼yd (1.25m) in total – you will need a 9in (23cm) square of each colour plus extra for other shapes in the star, background areas and borders
- Backing fabric 1⅓yd (1.3m)
- Wadding (batting) 47in x 47in (119cm x 119cm)
- Binding strips 174in (442cm) x 1½in (3.8cm), or the width you prefer
- Quilting threads as desired
- Square cutting ruler 6in–8in with diagonal line

Quilt Blocks Cutting Chart

This chart is for a 21⁵⁄₁₆in (54cm) finished block. The chart excludes the two-triangle Feather Squares made using bias-strip piecing – see step 1 on page 102 for cutting details. For border fabric pieces – see the Borders Cutting Chart below. Templates are on page 107.

Fabric	Shape	Template number	Number needed	Squares to cut	Cut size of square	Additional cut
Assorted lights	▱	D1	8		Use template on page 107	
	△	TT1	8	2	3in x 3in (7.62cm x 7.62cm)	⊠
	◺	T3	4	2	4⁵⁄₈in x 4⁵⁄₈in (11.8cm x 11.8cm)	◹
	△	TT3	4	1	6½in x 6½in (16.5cm x 16.5cm)	⊠
	▱	T5	8		Use template on page 107	
Assorted mediums	◹	T2	4	2	3⁷⁄₁₆in x 3⁷⁄₁₆in (8.8cm x 8.8cm)	◹
	△	TT2	4	1	4⁷⁄₈in x 4⁷⁄₈in (12.4cm x 12.4cm)	⊠
	▲	T4	8		Use template on page 107	
Assorted darks	■	S1	8	8	1¾in x 1¾in (4.44cm x 4.44cm)	
	◢	T2	4	2	3⁷⁄₁₆in x 3⁷⁄₁₆in (8.8cm x 8.8cm)	◹
	▲	TT2	4	1	4⁷⁄₈in x 4⁷⁄₈in (12.4cm x 12.4cm)	⊠
	◥	T3	4	2	4⁵⁄₈in x 4⁵⁄₈in (11.8cm x 11.8cm)	◹

Borders Cutting Chart

* Border strips are made from random length rectangles 4¼in (10.8cm) wide, sewn end to end to the length required. Templates are on page 107.

Fabric	Shape	Template number	Number needed	Squares to cut	Cut size of square	Additional cut
Lights	Border strips	See * above	4		4¼in x 33⁵⁄₈in (10.8cm x 85.4cm)	
	⏢	A	8	8 rectangles	4⁷⁄₈in x 15½in (12.4cm x 39.37cm)	See Fig 25
	◺	T3	8	4	4⁵⁄₈in x 4⁵⁄₈in (11.75cm x 11.75cm)	◹
Darks	▲	TT1	8	2	3in x 3in (7.6cm x 7.6cm)	⊠
	▲	TT3	4	1	6½in x 6½in (16.5cm x 16.5cm)	⊠

Tip

When sewing Feathered Star together refer often to the diagrams as it is easy to reverse colours or directions. Stitch the smallest pieces together first to form units. Join smaller units to form larger ones until blocks are complete.

*"The unique geometry of the traditional Le Moyne or
Eight-Pointed Star and the inspiration of an antique quilt,
gave rise to this original design."*

Bias-strip piecing the feathers

I use bias-strip piecing to make the smallest triangle units or feather squares in the Feathered Star blocks. Each feather square is made of two triangles but is actually cut as a square. In this method, large beginning squares of fabric are cut into bias strips, which are then sewn together. Squares are then each cut with the seam line centred corner to corner. Because seams are initially sewn on bias edges, the cut squares have the straight grain on the outer edges, which means that these edges do not stretch. All measurements include ¼in (6mm) seam allowance. Cut and piece the two-triangle square units for the centre star and sawtooth border using this bias-strip piecing technique described below.

1 Cut ten 9in (22.86in) beginning squares of assorted light fabrics and ten 9in (22.86in) beginning squares of assorted coloured fabrics. Layer light and coloured fabrics with right sides facing to make ten sets. For each set of squares, make a diagonal cut corner to corner across the squares to establish the true bias (45 degree angle) (Fig 2).

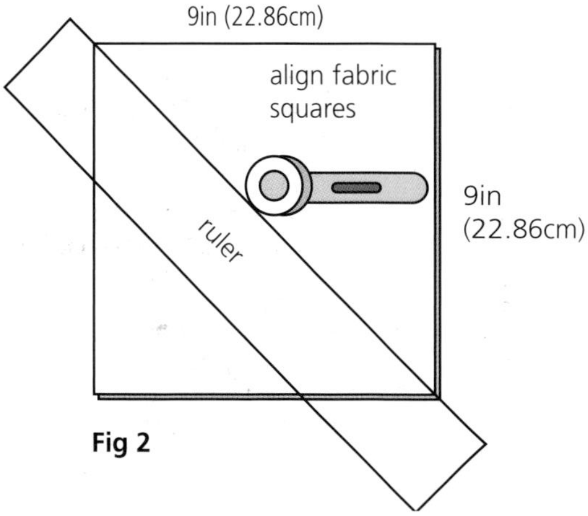

Fig 2

Tip

When piecing Feathered Star designs organize your sewing to save time and avoid confusion. Lay the cut patches for your star out on the sewing table in the design to make sure all the patches have been cut and to check the colour arrangement. Then separate the patches into the major piecing units: the centre, the side units and the corner units. The sides and corners can be stacked four layers deep to maximize chain piecing and help keep mirror image feather units in the proper places.

2 Measuring from the centre cut, cut strips 2in (5cm) wide (Fig 3). There will be four sets of strips (two long and two short) plus corner triangles (Fig 4).

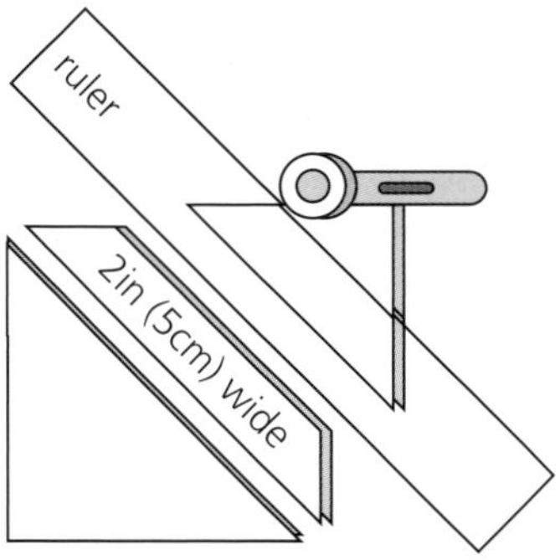

Fig 3

Fig 4

3 Pick up pairs of contrasting strips – they will be right sides together and ready to stitch. Sew them together on the long bias edge, using a ¼in (6mm) seam. Press seams open (Fig 5).

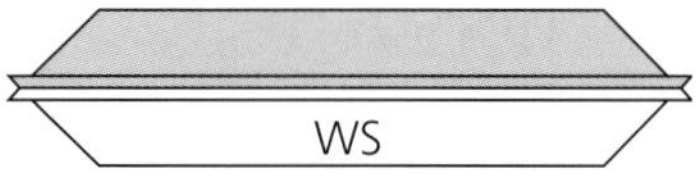

Fig 5

4 Sew strip pairs together as shown in Fig 6. Sew the long strip pairs together, and then the short. Keep the 'Vs' along the bottom edge even. Corner triangles left over after cutting strips can also be sewn together. Press all seams open.

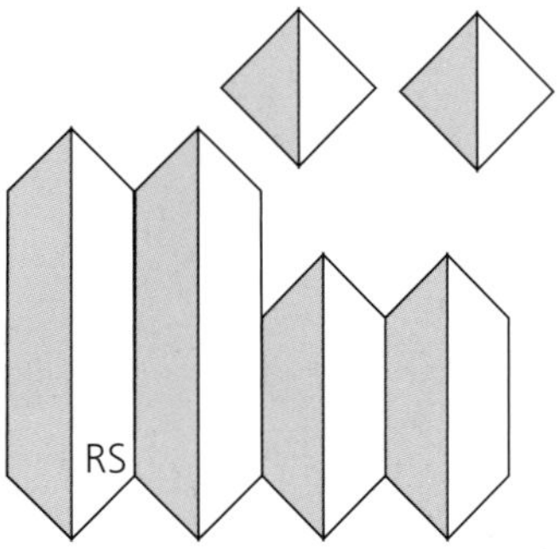

Fig 6

5 From each strip set-up, cut nine Feather Squares 2in x 2in (5cm x 5cm) for the sawtooth border and cut nine Feather Squares 1¾in x 1¾in (4.4cm x 4.4cm) for the centre block. Fig 7 shows the order and sizes of the squares to cut – 84 squares of each size are needed (there will be a few extra).

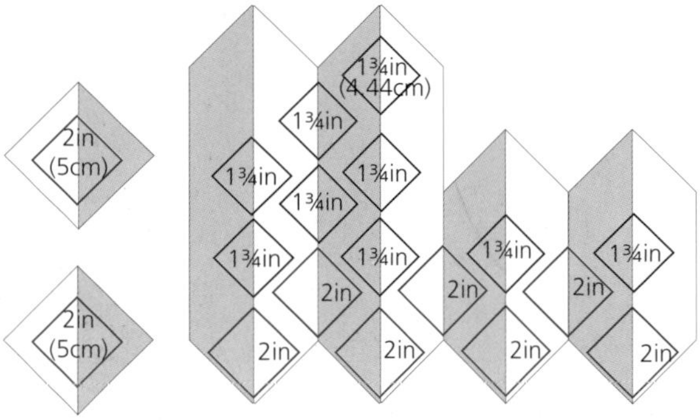

Fig 7

6 Using a square cutting ruler and rotary cutter, begin cutting the first row of Feather Squares at the lowest points as in Fig 8. Place the diagonal line of the ruler on the first seam line. Cut squares slightly (a few threads to ⅛in/3mm) larger than the desired cut size of the Feather Square. Two cuts are required to separate the square from the sewn strips (see Tip below). Cut squares from alternate seam lines working across the strips from one side to the other. After cutting the first set of squares, go back and cut from the skipped seam lines. Continue until all the needed squares are cut (Fig 9).

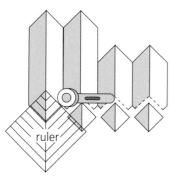

Fig 8 First row of squares   **Fig 9** Second row of squares

When cutting the Feather Squares, let your rotary cutter go a few threads beyond the seam line on each cut to cleanly separate the square without leaving a maddening two threads uncut.

7 The squares cut from the strips now must be cut to the exact size desired. Turn each square so the two sides that were just cut are pointing towards you. Align the diagonal line of the square rotary cutting ruler with the seam line of the square and the exact dimension on the ruler with the cut sides of the square. Make the final two cuts (Fig 10).

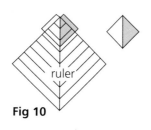

Fig 10

When sewing the feather rows, sew with the rows on top so the points can be clearly seen. Fig 11 shows the appearance of seams that are pressed open on the rows of feathers. Stitch right through the point indicated for crisp feather triangle points.

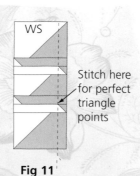

Fig 11

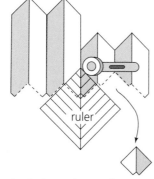

Piecing the centre Le Moyne Star

1 The finished Le Moyne Star is shown in Fig 12. Start by cutting the fabric pieces needed for the star according to the Quilt Blocks Cutting Chart on page 100. See the Tip on page 106 for advice on set-in seams (where three seams come together in a Y shape). Use the templates D1, T2 and TT2 on page 107.

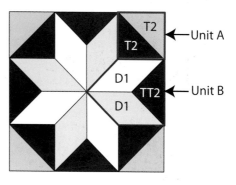

Fig 12 Le Moyne Star block – make 1

2 Lay the cut pieces out to determine which to sew together first. Make Unit A by sewing two T2 triangles together. Press seams towards the medium-coloured fabric. Make four of Unit A (Fig 13).

Fig 13 Unit A – make 4

3 Now make Unit B (see Fig 14). Start by sewing a diamond D1 to a triangle T2. With the triangle on top, begin to sew at the ¼in (6mm) seam line. Mark the starting point with a marking pen. Backtack by sewing two stitches forward and two stitches back, taking care not to stitch into the seam allowance. Sew the remainder of the seam, ending at the cut edge of the fabric. (No backtack is necessary here as the seam will be crossed and held by another.)

Fig 14 Unit B – make 4

Tip

When matching the triangle to the diamond in the first step of making Unit B, match the 45 degree angle edges of the two shapes. The 90 degree corner of the triangle will extend slightly beyond the diamond (see Fig 15).

Fig 15 ← match   corner will extend

4 Now sew the second diamond to the same triangle. With the triangle on top, sew from the outside edge of the fabric, ending with a backtack at the ¼in (6mm) seam line. Folding the triangle out of the way, match the points of the diamond to position them for the third seam. Stitch the diamonds together, beginning with a backtack at the inner ¼in (6mm) seam line and ending at the raw edge of the fabric.

5 With an iron, gently press the centre seam open. Press the other two seams toward the diamonds. Make four of Unit B in this way.

6 Now make Unit C by sewing a Unit A to a Unit B (see Fig 16). With Unit A on top, begin stitching with a backtack at the inner ¼in (6mm) seam line and sew to the outside raw edge. You need four of Unit C.

Fig 16 Unit C– make 4

7 You should now have the four Unit Cs that make up the star (see Fig 17a). Join two units together (Fig 17b), first matching the square of one Unit C to the diamond of the next. With the square on top, stitch from the outside edge, ending with a backtack at the inner ¼in (6mm) seam line. To sew the diamonds together, match the points, folding the rest of the piecing out of the way. Use a positioning pin to match the centre seams. Pin normally and remove the positioning pin. Beginning with a backtack, stitch from the inner ¼in (6mm) seam line through the centre seams to the raw edge of the fabric. Press centre seams open and the corner-square seams towards the centre.

Fig 17a

Fig 17b

8 To finish the block will take three more seams. Follow the procedure as in step 7 to join the corner squares to diamonds joining the two Unit Cs. The final seam is the centre seam. Use a positioning pin to carefully match the diamonds at the centre point. Pin the seam securely and remove the positioning pin before stitching. Backtacking at the ¼in (6mm) seam line, stitch precisely through the centre, ending with another backtack at the ¼in (6mm) seam. Press the centre seam open and the remaining seams towards the centre to complete the Le Moyne star (Fig 17c).

Fig 17c

Piecing the side units

1 Refer to Fig 18 for the complete layout. Begin by making four side units as follows. Join T4 and T5 triangles to make eight kite-shaped units (Fig 19).

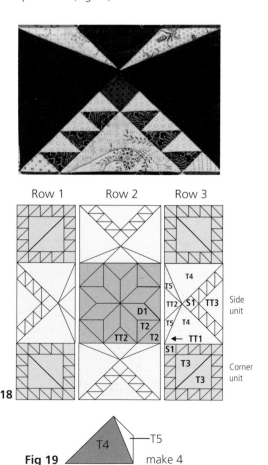

Fig 18

Fig 19   make 4

2 Piece feather rows as described on page 102, steps 1–7. See also the Tip and diagram at the bottom of page 103. Stitch feather rows to TT3 outside triangles (Fig 20). Now join kite shapes and triangles as shown Fig 21a and 21b. Make four side units in total.

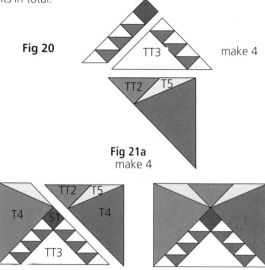

Fig 20   make 4

Fig 21a
make 4

Fig 21b Side unit – make 4

Piecing the corner units

Make four corner units as follows. Stitch T3 triangles together to make four squares (Fig 22). Complete the feather rows, with an S1 square in the bottom right corner and then join to the T3 unit as in Fig 23.

Fig 22

Fig 23 Corner unit – make 4

Assembling the central panel

Join the sewn units together in rows as follows (see Fig 18).
Row 1 corner unit + side unit + corner unit.
Row 2 side unit + Le Moyne Star block + side unit.
Row 3 corner unit + side unit + corner unit.
Stitch the three rows together to complete the central panel.

Piecing the borders

1 Start by cutting the fabric patches according to the Borders Cutting Chart on page 100.

2 Border 1: use the remaining 1¾in (4.4cm) Feather Squares to make four triangle sections (Fig 24). Follow Fig 25 to create a trapezium-shaped template and cut eight in your light fabric. Join a trapezium shape A to each side of the pieced triangle section (Fig 26). Note that Border 1 involves a set-in seam at each corner – see Tip below.

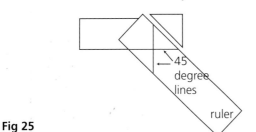

Fig 24 – make 4
TT3 TT1

Fig 25

Fig 26 Border 1 – make 4

Tip

Set-in seams are intersections of three pieces of fabric, where the seams form a Y shape. Set-in seams are needed to make the centre Le Moyne Star and the larger trapezoid background pieces. In general, where three seams come together in a Y, stop all stitching at the ¼in (6mm) seam line and backtack. I mark these points on the wrong side of the fabric. Don't let even one stitch extend beyond the marked seam allowance. As each seam is finished, take the work out of the sewing machine, position the next seam, and start stitching in the new direction. Backtacking is necessary because these seams will not be crossed and held by any other stitches.

3 Border 2: join the 2in (5cm) Feather Squares to create four rows as shown in Fig 27.

make 2

make 2

Fig 27 Border 2

4 Border 3: use the light T3 triangles to make four squares as in Fig 28. Join these sewn units to each end of two 4¼in (10.8cm) wide border strips (Fig 29).

Fig 28 – make 4

Fig 29 Border 3

5 Join the border sections to the centre panel as in Fig 30. Note that Border 1 involves a set-in seam at each corner.

Fig 30

Finishing the quilt

The quilt top now needs to be layered with the wadding and backing fabric (see page 112). The design can then be quilted by hand or machine as desired – mine was machine quilted by Barbara Ford. Bind the quilt to finish (see page 114).

"Take your time with this design. Use your best skills and you will have a quilt you can be proud of."

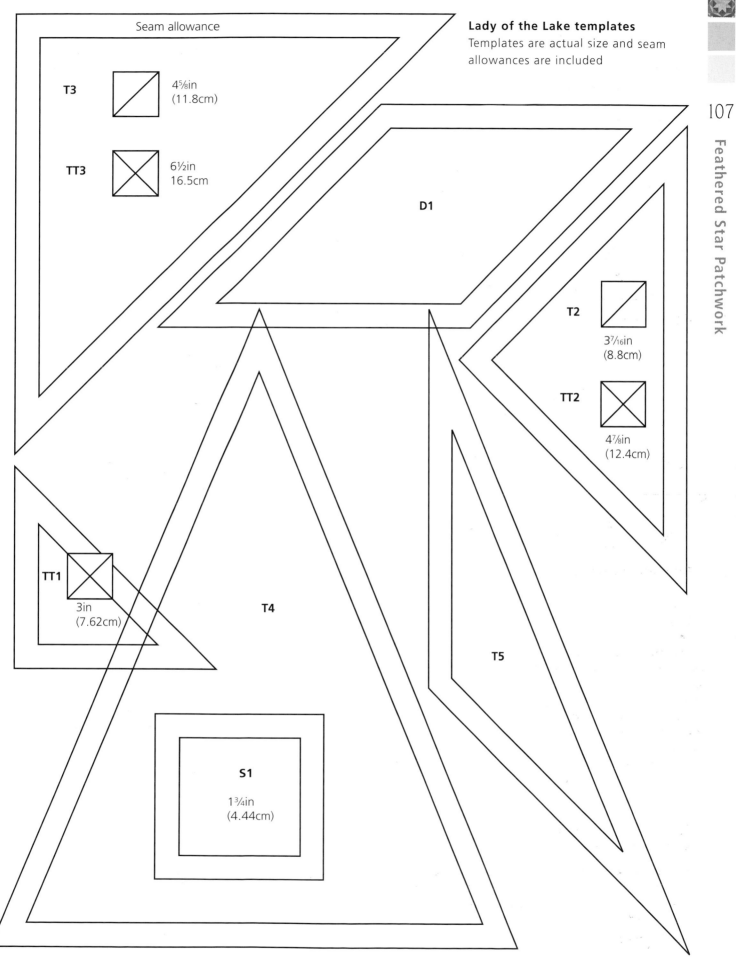

Seam allowance

T3 4⅝in (11.8cm)

TT3 6½in 16.5cm

D1

T2 3⁷⁄₁₆in (8.8cm)

TT2 4⅞in (12.4cm)

TT1 3in (7.62cm)

T4

T5

S1 1¾in (4.44cm)

General Techniques

Instructions for making the quilts in this book are contained in each chapter but some general techniques relevant to most of the quilts are described in this section, along with advice on patchwork and quilting tools you will need.

Tools

Many of the projects in this book require rotary cutting equipment. You will need a self-healing cutting mat at least 28in x 24in (72cm x 60cm) and a rotary cutter. The 45mm or the 60mm rotary cutter is recommended.

Any rotary cutting work requires rulers and most people have a make they prefer. The markings need to be clear and accurate and the ruler should preferably have a non-slip finish. If your ruler doesn't have a non-slip finish it is important to add fabric grips that will stabilize the ruler when in use. A 6½in x 24in (16cm x 60cm) basic ruler is recommended, plus a large square no less than 12½in (32cm), which is handy for squaring up and making sure you are always cutting at right angles.

The bias strip piecing method used in the Lady of the Lake quilt on page 100 requires a 6in–8in (15.2cm–20.3cm) square cutting ruler with a diagonal line.

Pinning

Don't underestimate the benefits of pinning. When you have to align a seam it is important to insert pins to stop any movement when sewing. Long, fine pins with flat heads are recommended as they will go through the layers of fabric easily and allow you to sew up to and over them.

Seams should always be pressed in opposite directions so they will nest together nicely, except where indicated otherwise in the project instructions. Insert a pin either at right angles or diagonally through the seam intersection, ensuring that the seams are matching perfectly. When sewing, do not remove the pin too early as your fabric might shift and your seams will then not be perfectly aligned.

Seams

It is very important to maintain an accurate ¼in (6mm) seam allowance throughout, unless otherwise stated in the project instructions. Using a *scant* ¼in seam will allow for the thickness of thread and the tiny amount of fabric taken up when the seam is pressed. These are both extremely small amounts but if they are ignored you will find your exact ¼in seam allowance is taking up more than ¼in.

Seam allowance test

It is well worth testing your seam allowance before starting on a quilt and most sewing machines have various needle positions that can be used to make any adjustments.

- Take a 2½in strip and cut off three segments 1½in wide (see Fig 1a below).
- Sew two segments together down the longer side and press the seam to one side (Fig 1b).
- Sew the third segment across the top – it should fit exactly (Fig 1c). If it doesn't, you need to make an adjustment to your seam allowance. If it is too long, your seam allowance is too wide and can be corrected by moving the needle on your sewing machine to the right. If it is too small, your seam allowance is too narrow and this can be corrected by moving the needle to the left.

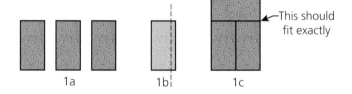

This should fit exactly

1a   1b   1c

Fig 1a, 1b and 1c Seam allowance test

Chain Piecing

Chain piecing is the technique of feeding a series of fabric pieces through the sewing machine without lifting the presser foot and without cutting the thread between each piece (see Fig 2). Always chain piece when you can as it saves time and thread. Once your chain is complete simply snip the thread between the pieces.

When chain piecing shapes other than squares and rectangles it is sometimes preferable when finishing one shape, to lift the presser foot slightly and reposition on the next shape but still leaving the thread uncut.

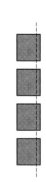

Fig 2 Chain piecing

Pressing

In quiltmaking, pressing is of vital importance and if extra care is taken you will be well rewarded.

- Always set your stitches after sewing by pressing the seam as sewn (Fig 3a). This eases any tension and prevents the seam line from distorting. Move the iron with an up and down motion, zigzagging along the seam rather than ironing down the length of the seam.
- Open up your pieced fabric and press on the right side of the fabric towards the darker fabric (Fig 3b), if necessary guiding the seam underneath to make sure the seam is going in the right direction. Press with an up and down motion.
- Always take care if using steam and certainly don't use steam anywhere near a bias edge or it could stretch and distort.
- Each seam must be pressed flat before another seam is sewn across it. Unless there is a special reason for not doing so, seams are pressed towards the darker fabric. The main criteria when joining seams, however, is to have the seam allowances going in the opposite direction to each other as they then nest together without bulk. Your patchwork will lie flat and your seam intersections will be accurate.

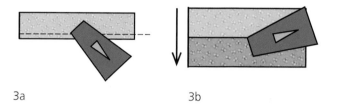

3a   3b

Fig 3a and 3b Pressing

Dog Ears

A dog ear is the excess piece of fabric that overlaps past the seam allowance when sewing triangles to other shapes. Dog ears should always be cut off to reduce bulk. They can be trimmed using a rotary cutter although snipping with small, sharp scissors is quicker. Make sure you are trimming the points parallel to the straight edge of the triangle (see Fig 4).

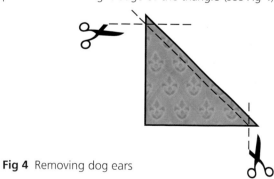

Fig 4 Removing dog ears

Using Templates

If you are using templates to make your blocks, as some of the projects in this book do, a template will be needed for each different shape used in the blocks. Templates should be made from template plastic and they should include a ¼in (6mm) seam allowance all round. Some projects already include a seam allowance on the templates – refer to the project instructions. Wherever possible templates have been produced at full size.

- Mark each template with the name of the block, its finished size and an identifying letter. Do this on the right side of the template so that you have an instant check on which way up it should be. This is particularly necessary with asymmetric shapes.
- It is also extremely useful to mark each template with an arrow to show the direction of the fabric grain line.
- Keep organized and store all the templates for a particular block together, labelled with the name and size plus a drawing of the block, with each patch lettered.
- To cut out your fabric from the template, lay the pressed fabric out flat, wrong side up (iron the fabric first if necessary). Place the template face down on the fabric, wherever possible lining up the arrow on the template with the fabric grain. Do not include a selvedge, either in a patch or its seam allowance, unless otherwise instructed in the individual project instructions. Use a hard lead pencil and draw around the template carefully, taking particular care at points and corners.
- For the most economical use of fabric, cut the patches close together unless you want to 'fussy cut' a particular piece or motif, in which case place the template over that particular area of the fabric.

Reversing templates

For some techniques, such as fusible web applique, template shapes need to be reversed. The easiest way to reverse a template from this book is to photocopy it and then, using a light source such as a window or a lightbox, place the copy on to the surface with the template face down. Trace the now reversed template on to the paper side of your fusible web or template plastic.

Another method is to trace the template on to tracing paper and then turn the tracing paper over and trace the template on to the paper side of your fusible web from the wrong side of the tracing paper.

Appliqué

Appliqué is a technique where pieces of fabric are attached to a background fabric and there are various ways to do this. Two methods are described here – appliqué using fusible web bing and the more traditional sewn approach where the fabric edges are turned under (often called needleturn appliqué). If using fusible webbing, make sure that the templates you are using have been reversed, because you will be drawing the shape on the back of the fabric.

Fusible web appliqué

Fusible webbing is a very useful product that allows one piece of fabric to be fused to another. The thin webbing of glue melts under the heat of a hot iron. See the individual manufacturer's instructions for use.

1 Reverse the templates, as described on page 109. Trace around each shape on to the paper side of the fusible webbing, leaving about ½in (1.3cm) around each shape.

2 Cut out roughly around each shape (there is no need to be accurate at this point). Iron the fusible webbing on to the wrong side of the appropriate fabrics, paper side up, and cut out accurately on the line.

3 When cool, peel the backing paper from the piece of fusible webbing. Using the quilt photograph as a guide or your own judgement, position the appliqué shape and press into place with a hot iron. The manufacturer's instructions will indicate how long to press but about ten seconds or so is usually enough. Allow the patch to cool.

4 Using two strands of embroidery thread, blanket stitch (see page 115) around the edges of the appliqué.

A fusible web appliquéd motif with a blanket stitch edging.

Traditional (needle-turn) appliqué

1 Make templates from template plastic for the required shapes. Using an appropriate marking pen (such as a vanishing marker or water-soluble one), trace around the templates on the wrong side of the appropriate fabrics and cut out leaving a ¼in (6mm) seam allowance.

2 Fold the raw edge to the wrong side of the fabric, using the marked line as a guide. Tack (baste) in place and press. Remember to clip any concave curves (these are the curves that go in) so they sit neatly.

3 Once the edges are turned under and tacked (basted), spray with water to remove any marks and then press the shapes, first on the wrong side and then on the right side. Now stitch the appliqué shapes in position using a blind hem stitch (see page 116), using thread that matches the background fabric so it doesn't show.

Joining Strips

If you need to join strips for your borders and binding, join them with a diagonal seam to make them less noticeable (see Fig 5). Press the seams open.

Fig 5 Joining strips of fabric

Adding Straight Borders

When adding borders to a square quilt it doesn't matter if you add the sides first and then the top and bottom or vice versa, just be consistent, or follow the project instructions. If putting straight borders on a rectangular quilt it is the custom to add the longest borders first, or follow the project instructions.

1 Determine the vertical measurement of your quilt top from top to bottom through the centre. Cut two side border strips to this measurement.

2 Mark the halves and quarters of one quilt side and one border with pins (Fig 6a). Placing right sides together and matching the pins, stitch the quilt and border together, easing the quilt side to fit where necessary (Fig 6b). Repeat on the opposite side. Remove pins and press seams open.

3 Now determine the horizontal measurement from side to side across the centre of the quilt top, including the borders you have just added. Cut two top and bottom border strips to this measurement and add to the quilt top in the same manner as before (Fig 6c).

4 Lift the side border above the top border and fold it to align with the top border. Press it to create a 45 degree line (Fig 7b). Repeat with all four corners.

5 Align the horizontal and vertical borders in one corner by folding the quilt diagonally and stitch along the pressed 45 degree line to form the mitre, back stitching at either end. Trim the excess border fabric ¼in (6mm) from your sewn line. Repeat with the other three corners.

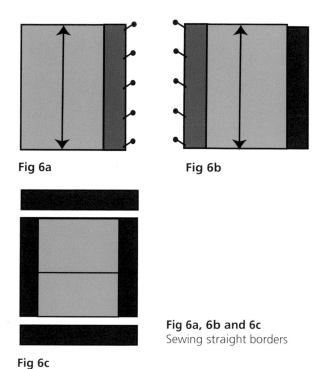

Fig 6a   **Fig 6b**

Fig 6a, 6b and 6c
Sewing straight borders

Fig 6c

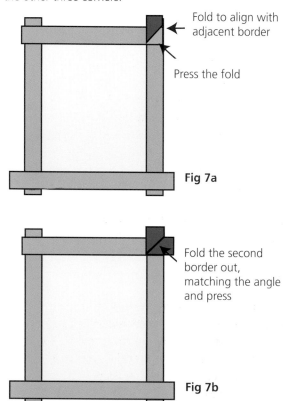

Fold to align with adjacent border

Press the fold

Fig 7a

Fold the second border out, matching the angle and press

Fig 7b

Fig 7a and 7b Sewing mitred borders

Adding Mitred Borders

1 Measure the length and width of the quilt and cut two border strips the length of the quilt plus twice the width of the border and then cut two border strips the width of the quilt plus twice the width of the border.

2 Sew the border strips to the quilt beginning and ending ¼in (6mm) away from the corners, back stitching to secure at either end. Begin your sewing right next to where you have finished sewing your previous border but ensure your stitching doesn't overlap. When you have sewn your four borders, press and lay the quilt out on a flat surface, with the reverse side of the quilt upwards (see Fig 7a).

3 Following Fig 7a, fold the top border up and align it with the side border. Press the resulting 45 degree line that starts at the ¼in (6mm) stop and runs to the outside edge of the border.

A mitred border not only looks neat but is ideal if you are showcasing an attractive fabric, such as this pretty rose print.

Quilting

Quilting stitches hold the patchwork top, wadding (batting) and backing together and create texture over your finished patchwork. There are many brands and varieties of wadding to choose from and this is very much a personal taste. Polyester wadding will wash well but if you like the antique effect that old quilts have then a cotton wadding, which will shrink a little on washing, will give you that effect. Your local quilting store will be happy to advise you. You can choose to hand quilt or machine quilt or, if time is at a premium, you can send the quilt off to a longarm quilting service.

Marking your quilt

If you need to mark a quilting design on your top this must be done before joining the three layers together. Quilting designs can be taken from numerous books or you can use stencils, and these patterns must be marked on the right side of your quilt top. There are many marking pens and pencils available but whatever you decide to use, it is very important to test it first to ensure it will not permanently mark the fabric. Use a fine marker, or keep your pencil sharp, the secret being only to mark as much as necessary to enable you to see the design. If using a water-erasable marker remember to remove the marks before pressing otherwise you may set the lines.

Joining the layers

Joining the layers of quilt top, wadding and backing is often called making a quilt sandwich.

1 Lay the backing fabric right side down on a smooth surface and tape the corners to hold the fabric down flat. Lay the wadding (batting) on top, taking care to smooth out any wrinkles. Lay the quilt top right side up centrally on top.

2 Tack (baste) the three layers together in a grid, starting in the centre and working out to the edges. The rows of tacking (basting) should be about 6in (15.2cm) apart. Alternatively, if you are machine quilting, the three layers can be pin basted using 1in (2.5cm) safety pins, again every 6in (15.2cm) or so, avoiding placing the pins on any marked quilting lines. Do not use safety pins if you are hand quilting as the pins may well have to stay in the fabric for some time and could cause damaging marks on your quilt top.

Hand Quilting

You can hand quilt on a frame, in a quilting hoop or just in your lap. You will need quilting thread, betweens needles, small scissors and a thimble. Betweens needles are shorter and finer than regular needles and will help you produce smaller quilting stitches.

The quilting stitch is a simple running stitch. It is more important to have straight stitches of equal length and spacing than to have tiny, uneven stitches. A good target to aim for is to have about ten stitches to 1in (2.5cm) ideally, the stitches on the back should be the same size as those on the top. Start quilting in the centre of the quilt and work outwards.

1 To begin quilting, thread a needle with approximately 18in (46cm) of quilting thread, knot it and insert the needle from the top into the wadding (batting) a short distance from where you plan to start. Bring the needle out at the starting point. Tug lightly on the thread to pop the knot into the wadding. You are aiming to make it impossible to tell where the quilting line begins and ends.

2 Have a thimble on the middle finger of your right hand (reverse if you are left-handed). The hand with the thimble is your sewing hand and stays on top of the quilt, the other hand stays below the quilt. The index finger of this hand should also be protected. Holding the needle perpendicular to the quilt or at a very slight angle, push it through the fabric with the top of the thimble until you can just feel the point with your left index finger. To bring the needle back to the top, press the eye of the needle flat against the quilt with the thimble while pushing the point of the needle up with your left index finger. After practising you should be able to put several stitches on your needle before pulling it all the way through the fabric.

3 To end the quilting, tie a knot a short distance from your work, make a final stitch through the top and the wadding (batting) and out again a needle length or two away, then pull the knot through to the inside of the wadding and cut the thread.

Hand quilting not only adds texture and interest but can echo the colours of the fabrics. You can choose from many different types of thread.

Big-stitch quilting

Big-stitch quilting is also a hand quilting technique, which gives a more naïve and primitive look to a quilt. Thicker thread is used and although it is also a running stitch, the stitches are larger and you are not necessarily aiming at perfectly even stitches. Perle cotton thread or cotton à broder are good threads to use and you can use a number 5 between needle, which has a larger eye, or use a crewel embroidery needle.

Machine Quilting

You can machine quilt with most sewing machines although you do need a walking foot for straight line quilting and you must be able to drop the feed dogs for free-motion quilting. Thread your bobbin with a good quality thread in a colour to match your backing. Normally, the top thread should match your quilt top. Quilting 'in the ditch' means straight line machine quilting between seams or very close to seam lines.

Straight line machine quilting

Straight line machine quilting is only successful if you have a walking foot or an even-feed foot, which will feed both the top and the bottom layers evenly through the machine. Many new sewing machines have this facility.

Place your machine on a large table so that the quilt is supported at the side and the back while it is being stitched. Starting at one side, roll the quilt towards the centre up to the start of the quilting. Secure the roll tightly with clips to enable it to go neatly under the head of the machine. Quilt a central line from the top to the bottom of the quilt. Unroll the quilt to the next quilting line and quilt. Continue in this way until you reach the edge and then roll from the opposite side and quilt in the same manner.

Free-motion machine quilting

This method allows you to stitch curved and intricate quilting patterns on your machine. Use a darning foot and drop the feed dogs so that you will be able to move the quilt in any direction without having to turn it. If you are new to free-motion quilting, an embroidery hoop is useful to keep the fabric flat and provide the right amount of fabric tension. Without the feed dogs, the stitch length is controlled by how fast or how slowly you move the quilt through the machine. The aim is to produce small, even stitches. Practise on a spare piece of fabric until you are happy with the result.

Machine quilting a simple grid pattern can look most effective, as well as provide background texture, as you can see in this detail picture from the Country-Style Welcome quilt. Echo quilting is also used to outline the flowers in the gorgeous border.

The patterns available via longarm quilting and free-motion quilting are almost limitless and can add the perfect finishing touch to a quilt.

Binding your Quilt

A double-fold French binding gives a professional finish to your quilt whether you are using straight or bias binding. If your quilt has curved edges you must use bias binding, but if your quilt has straight sides you can use either straight or bias binding. Cut your binding strips 2½in (6.3cm) wide, or to the measurement stated in the individual project instructions.

1 Trim the excess backing and wadding (batting) so that the edges are even with the top of the quilt.

2 Join your binding strips into a continuous length (see Fig 5 on page 110), making sure there is sufficient to go around the quilt plus 8in–10in (20.3cm–25.4cm) for the corners and for overlapping ends. With wrong sides together, press the binding in half lengthways. Fold and press under ½in (1.3cm) to neaten the edge at the end where you will start sewing.

3 On the right side of the quilt and starting around 12in (30cm) away from a corner, align the edges of the double thickness binding with the edge of the quilt so that the cut edges are towards the edges of the quilt, and pin to hold in place (Fig 8a). Sew with a ¼in (6mm) seam allowance, leaving the first 1in (2.5cm) open.

4 At the first corner, stop ¼in (6mm) from the edge of the fabric and backstitch (Fig 8a). Lift the needle and presser foot and fold as shown Fig 8b, then fold again as shown in Fig 8c. Stitch from the edge to ¼in (6mm) from the next corner and repeat the turn. Continue all around the quilt working each corner in the same way. When you come to the starting point, cut the binding, fold under the cut edges and overlap at the starting point.

5 Now fold over the binding to the back of the quilt and hand stitch in place all round, pinning first if you prefer. At each corner fold the binding to form a neat mitre.

Labelling your Quilt

When you have finished your quilt it is important to label it even if the information you put on the label is just your name and the date. When looking at antique quilts it is always interesting to piece together information about the quilt so you can be sure that any extra information you put on your label will be of immense interest to quilters of the future. A very simple method of labelling is to write on a piece of calico with a permanent marker pen and then sew or appliqué this to the back of your quilt.

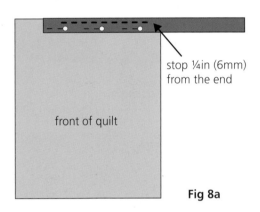

stop ¼in (6mm) from the end

front of quilt

Fig 8a

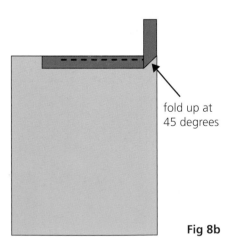

fold up at 45 degrees

Fig 8b

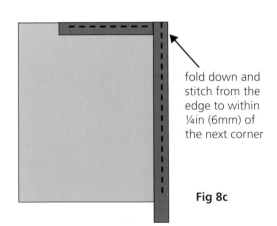

fold down and stitch from the edge to within ¼in (6mm) of the next corner

Fig 8c

Fig 8a, 8b and 8c
Binding the quilt

Decorative Stitches

Some of the quilts in this book use decorative stitches to add extra interest and texture. Some common stitches are provided here as diagrams.

Backstitch

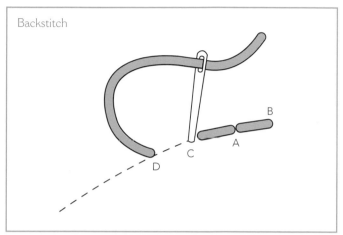

Blanket stitch

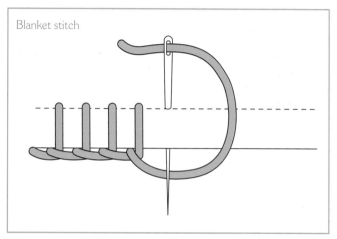

Chain stitch

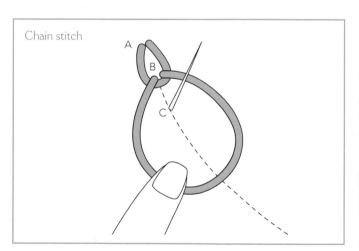

Feather stitch

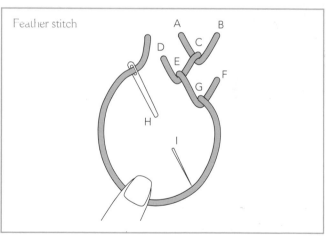

French knot

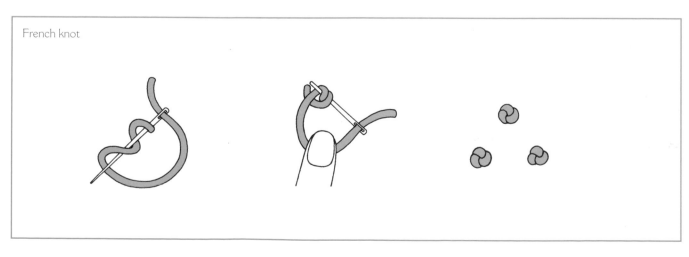

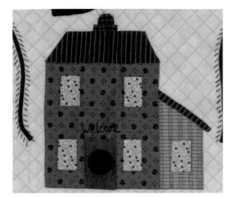

Hemming stitch

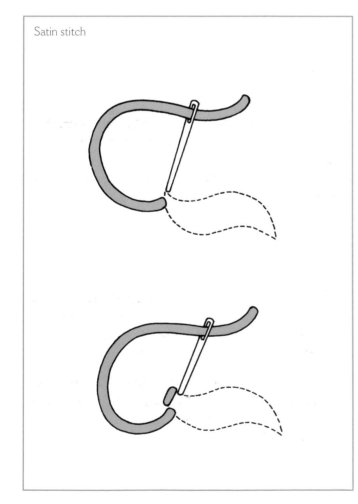

Satin stitch

Herringbone stitch

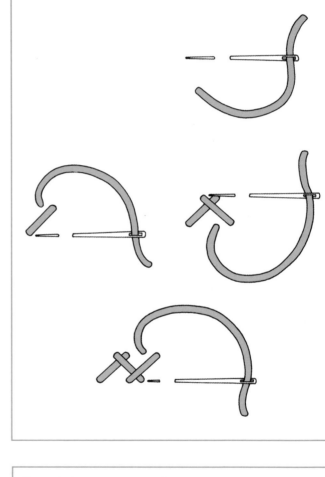

Stem stitch

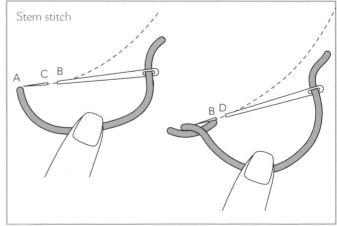

A C B

B D

Suppliers

Lynette Anderson Designs
Wholesale enquiries to Creative Abundance, PO Box 7244, Upper Ferntree Gully, Victoria 3156, Australia.
Tel: (+613) 9753 5479
Fax: (+613) 9758 4284
Email: nel@creativeabundance.com.au
www.lynetteandersondesigns.typepad.com

Creative Grids (UK) Ltd
Unit 1J, Peckleton Lane, Business Park, Peckleton,
Leicester, Leics LE9 7RN, UK
Tel: 01455 828667
www.creativegrids.com
For graph paper, drafting equipment and rotary rulers and cutters

Feathered Star Productions, Inc
1495 East 27th Avenue, Eugene, OR 97403, USA
Email: mccloskey1@aol.com
www.marshamccloskey.com

Henry Glass Fabrics
49 West 37th Street, New York 10018, USA

www.henryglassfabrics.com
For fabrics, including those of
Lynette Anderson-O'Rourke

Moda Fabrics/United Notions
13800 Hutton Drive, Dallas, Texas 75234, USA
www.modafabrics.com
Tel: 800-527-9447

The Quilt Room
20 West Street, Dorking, Surrey RH4 1BL, UK
Tel: 01306 740739
www.quiltroom.co.uk
For fabrics, threads, quilting supplies and longarm
quilting service

Thimbleberries, Inc
7 North Main Street, Hutchinson, MN 55350, USA
www.thimbleberries.com
For fabrics, quilt patterns, stencils and books
Quilting stencils by Quilting Creations International
are available from quilting shops or via
www.quiltingcreations.com

Acknowledgments

Lynne Edwards wishes to thank Kay Bruce, for sharing her freezer paper technique all those years ago.
Lynette Anderson-O'Rourke gives her thanks to Val, for her help with the hand sewing, and to Elizabeth for her wonderful machine quilting.

Joanna Figueroa would like to acknowledge Valerie Marsh for her wonderful and timely piecing and Diana Johnson for her amazing quilting.
Janet Bolton wishes to thank Pam Lintott for including her in the selection.

Additional Reading

Basic Beauties Big and Small (2009 Thimbleberries® ASIN B001TNNFCM)
Feathered Star Quilt Blocks I, Really Hard Blocks That Take a Long Time to Make Marsha McCloskey (2003 Feathered Star Productions Inc ISBN 0-9635422-9-1)
Fresh Vintage Sewing, Joanna Figueroa (2009 Martingale & Company ISBN 1564778940)
Pieced Borders: The Complete Resource Judy Martin and Marsha McCloskey (1994 Crosley-Griffith ISBN 0-929589-03-3)

Quilts and Coverlets Sheila Betterton (1978, ISBN: 0 9504971 4 2)
The Quilts of Gee's Bend: Masterpieces from a Lost Place William Arnett (2003, ISBN: 978-0965376648)
Mary Newcomb Christopher Andreae (2007, ISBN: 978-0853319597)
Old Swedish Quilts Asa Wettre (1995, ISBN: 978-1883010157)
Serizawa: Master of Japanese Textile Design Chosuke Serizawa (Edited By) (2001 Tohoku Fukushi University, Japan ISBN 4901459066)

About the Authors

Lynette Anderson-O'Rourke

Lynette's love affair with textiles began at a young age when her grandmother taught her to embroider and knit. Patchwork caught Lynette's attention in 1981 after the birth of her first son, and her affinity with textiles is apparent in her work. Moving with her family to Australia in 1990 prompted the release of Lynette first patterns in 1995 and during the ensuing years Lynette has produced hundreds of patterns. Lynette's distinctive, yet sophisticated naïve design style encompasses quilts, pillow, bags and sewing accessories. Her popular self-published books include, Bearly Stitched, Sunflower Stitching, An Angel's Wish, Friends For Christmas and Rainbow Cottage. Lynette was very excited when she was asked to join the team at Henry Glass Fabrics last year and launched her first fabrics lines in 2009. Visit her at www.lynetteandersondesigns.typepad.com

Janet Bolton

Janet Bolton was born in Lancashire, UK. During the 1960s she studied at the Harris School of Art, Preston, and Liverpool School of Art. Janet has written two books for children; *My Grandmother's Patchwork Quilt* and *Noah's Ark*, as well as a textbook on her appliqué and quilting techniques entitled *Patchwork Folk Art, In a Patchwork Garden* and *Textile Pictures*. Her work is represented in the collections of the Crafts Council, British Council and the Embroiderer's Guild. Since 1985 her work has featured in many exhibitions around the world including the Crafts Council, Contemporary Applied Arts, Robert Young Antiques, the Rona Gallery in London, the Works Gallery, Philadelphia, Gayle Wilson Gallery, The Hamptons, New York, Takeshimaya, Tokyo and the Museum De Stadshof, Holland. Janet has exhibited at Godfrey & Watt regularly since 1986. She now lives in London. Visit her at www.janetbolton.com

Lynne Edwards

Lynne Edwards teaches and demonstrates a wide range of patchwork and quilting techniques, both hand and machine. She has written several textbooks that are considered to be definitive works. Her previous books for David & Charles are: *The Sampler Quilt Book* (1996), *The New Sampler Quilt Book* (2000), *Making Scrap Quilts to Use It Up* (2003), *Stash-buster Quilts* (2006) and *Cathedral Window Quilts* (2008). In 1992 Lynne was awarded the Jewel Pearce Patterson Scholarship for International Quilt Teachers. This was in recognition of her outstanding qualities as a teacher and included a trip to the Houston Quilt Market and Festival. The award led to invitations to teach as part of the Houston Faculty in 1993 and 1995 and at the Symposium of the Australasian Quilters' Guild in Brisbane in 1993. In 2000, teaching commitments included Durban in South Africa and the National Canadian Festival, Canada in 2000. Lynne's long association with the quilting movement, both locally and nationally, has involved her in the organization of quilt shows – from local village halls to the Quilters' Guild National Exhibitions. She has served on selection committees and is an experienced judge of National Quilt Shows. She was Senior Judge at the South African Quilt Show in 1998, her first experience of judging overseas. In 2000, Lynne was given honorary lifetime membership of the Quilters' Guild of the British Isles, and in 2002 was awarded the Amy Emms Memorial Trophy for services to quilting. In 2008 Lynne was awarded an MBE for her services to arts and crafts.

Joanna Figueroa

Ever since she was a little girl Joanna remembers loving colour and creating. After stumbling upon quilting the same year she was married, she knew somehow she had found her favourite medium. Something about the total utilitarian and yet artistic quality of working with textiles won her over completely. Quilting quickly turned to teaching which evolved into pattern writing, books and designing fabric for Moda fabrics. She is currently working on her 16th fabric collection, has just released her second book and has self published over 100 patterns. When not sewing, writing or designing she loves to explore new towns, to work in her cottage garden, to read fiction about small towns and women's lives and most of all to spend time together as a family with her husband Eric, three kids (ages 4–11) and two beagles. You can visit her website at www.figtreeandco.com

Carolyn Forster

Over the years Carolyn's work has been featured in various British magazines including *Popular Patchwork, Fabrications* and *Patchwork & Quilting Magazine*. Her quilts have appeared on the television, both in the UK and in the USA, and she has contributed to books published by New Holland and That Patchwork Place. Carolyn has had a quilt hung for the Clothworks display at Quilt Market in the USA and recently designed projects for Makower fabrics. Her most recent endeavour has been to write the book, *Quilting-on-the-Go*, based on one of her most popular classes. Carolyn lives in Tunbridge Wells, Kent with her husband Craig and their son, who is not short of quilts on a chill winter's night! Catch up with Carolyn via her website blog at **www.carolynforster.co.uk**

Lynette Jensen

Classic designs and well-written instructions have made Lynette Jensen, founder of Thimbleberries, a leader in the international quilting community, an acclaimed fabric designer and a best-selling author. From her studio in the quaint country town of Hutchinson, Minnesota, Lynette has built one of the largest quilt pattern writing companies. Her look is defined by a traditional colour palette and upscale country style. Her generous spirit and bountiful ideas provide inspiration to those who share Lynette's passion for creating the pieces that make a house a home. In 2008 Thimbleberries celebrated twenty years of publishing patterns and books. Sixteen years ago, fabric was added to the brand and recently, thread for quilters, embroidery designs for computerized embroidery machines and stencils providing the quilter with everything needed to make a great quilt. Thimbleberries products are sold in thousands of quilt shops worldwide with a substantial portion of shops running exclusive Thimbleberries quilt clubs. A complete list of products can be found on **www.thimbleberries.com**

Marsha McCloskey

Marsha McCloskey is one of the quilting world's best-known authors and teachers. She has written or co-authored over twenty-five books on quiltmaking since 1981. Specializing in the Feathered Star and other traditional pieced designs, she has taught drafting, rotary cutting and machine piecing to quilters all over the United States and in nine foreign countries. Each year she travels about once a month to teach and lecture. She has her own small publishing company, Feathered Star Productions, Inc., a website, and has designed fabric for quilters since 1996. *Feathered Star Quilt Blocks I: Really Hard Blocks That Take a Long Time to Make* is her current book on Feathered Star designs, which has patterns for ten Le Moyne Star-based Feathered Star blocks. *Pieced Borders: The Complete Resource* by Judy Martin and Marsha McCloskey has 200 pieced border patterns with twelve complete quilt patterns. You can visit her website at **www.marshamccloskey.com**

Petra Prins

Petra Prins is one of those people that seems to have textiles in her genes. As a young girl she started designing and sewing clothes for her dolls and later for herself and her four children. After many years of being a high school teacher, she changed careers, starting a clothing shop where she made and sold her own designs. Patchwork and quilting was not very popular in the Netherlands in those days, but it was love at first sight when Petra was first introduced to it. During frequent visits to see her husband in the USA, she became more and more intrigued with antique quilts and it was there that she found the nineteenth century reproduction fabrics. She changed her business into 'Petra Prins Patchwork and Quilting' and it has grown ever since, known in Europe for quilt designs and a vast selection of reproduction fabrics including Japanese reproductions of antique French floral prints. Recently Petra's career has grown again with a new challenge. Together with best friend Nel Kooiman, they have taken over the famous Dutch store 'Den Haan & Wagenmakers' in Amsterdam. This store has been reproducing antique Dutch designs for more than 20 years. Making quilts combining English, American, French and Dutch reproduction fabrics. Petra's staff call her the 'Medallion Girl', as these quilts are her favourite, so for this book she designed a medallion quilt. It is her vision that a design should be simple: let the fabrics do their work! You can see more of her work on **www.dutchquilts.com** and **www.petraprinspatchwork.nl**

Index